COMMUNIST
INSURGENT

COMMUNIST INSURGENT

Blanqui's Politics of Revolution

Doug Enaa Greene

Haymarket Books
Chicago, Illinois

Published in 2017 by
Haymarket Books
P.O. Box 180165
Chicago, IL 60618
773-583-7884
www.haymarketbooks.org
info@haymarketbooks.org

ISBN: 978-1-60846-472-2

Trade distribution:
In the US, Consortium Book Sales and Distribution, www.cbsd.com
In Canada, Publishers Group Canada, www.pgcbooks.ca
In the UK, Turnaround Publisher Services, www.turnaround-uk.com
All other countries, Ingram Publisher Services International,
IPS_Intlsales@ingramcontent.com

This book was published with the generous support of Lannan
Foundation and Wallace Action Fund.

Printed in Canada by union labor.

Library of Congress Cataloging-in-Publication data is available.

2 4 6 8 10 9 7 5 3 1

*To my grandmother, for her unwavering support
and her willingness to always listen to me*

To Isla, my little buddy

CONTENTS

Acknowledgments

I didn't realize how collective writing a book was until I started this one. In the process of exploring the life and times of Louis-Auguste Blanqui, I have made many new friends and comrades. I also depended on the work of many others as I researched the life of L'Enfermé. I want to thank Mitchell Abidor, whose translations of Blanqui at the *Marxists Internet Archive* were my obvious starting point. I would also like to thank Ian Birchall, Boyd Nielson, and Gary Leupp for reading early drafts of my book and offering feedback. Peter Hallward and Philippe Le Goff's invaluable work creating the *Blanqui Archive* at Kingston University has made researching Blanqui much easier and contributed to a stronger book on my part. Thank you to Paul D'Amato for reading my first draft and sending me some sharp edits. This helped me far more than you know. Thanks to John MacDonald over at Haymarket for always being friendly answering all my questions. Finally, I owe a debt of gratitude to Richard Seymour for first putting me in contact with Haymarket and starting this whole process.

The following comrades and friends have also been constant sources of support. Forgive me if I miss anyone since there are so many of you: Amy Banelis, Jeffrey Baker, Francesca Gomes, Jennifer Harvey, Julia Pitt, Chris Persampieri, Joe Ramsey, and Fanshen Wong. To Ian Horst, when I say that you have a Blanquist heart, I mean it with the highest praise. Andrew and Christine Shelton, you are the best friends I've ever had. I especially want to thank Harrison

Fluss and Sam Miller, who are not only wonderful friends but also principled revolutionaries.

I owe a special debt to the following members of my family: my mother and grandmother for their tireless support. I want to thank Jocelyn and Mark for letting me stay with them when I was in London. To Danny and Lauren, I hope when you read this, you'll finally understand why this project consumed me.

Introduction

We all know what it really amounts to, this freedom that pleads against communism—it is the freedom to enslave, the freedom to exploit at will, the freedom of the great and the good . . . with the multitude as their stepping stone. This form of freedom is something that the people call oppression and crime. They no longer want to nourish it with their flesh and blood.
—**Louis-Auguste Blanqui**[1]

L ouis-Auguste Blanqui (1805–1881) was arguably the greatest French revolutionary and communist of the nineteenth century. His name stood for Jacobinism, republicanism, radical atheism, street fighting, barricades, insurrection, conspiracies, socialism, and communism. Over the course of his long life, Blanqui lived under six different French regimes—two empires, two republics, and two monarchies. He was the veteran of three revolutions and the organizer of a half-dozen abortive coup attempts. The price of Blanqui's revolutionary commitment was half a lifetime in prison enduring torture, disease, and deprivation. Blanqui's health was broken by these ordeals, and he was left for dead. Still, Blanqui survived every incarceration and emerged from the dungeons, refusing to compromise his mission of overthrowing capitalism.

Blanqui was born in the aftermath of the French Revolution and had to grapple with its unfulfilled promises of *liberté, égalité, fraternité*. The French Revolution had enabled the expansion of capitalism,

1

but for the workers it had not solved the problem of inequality and privilege. Blanqui was not indifferent to these questions. He came to believe that in order to liberate the workers and end capitalism, Jacobinism and other traditions born of 1789 were not enough. Socialism was the true heir to the French Revolution, and it alone took the side of the workers and was the solution of an enlightened and egalitarian society.

The speculation on how to organize a classless society that preoccupied the utopians of Blanqui's day did not interest him. He did not consider socialism to be a theoretical question but a practical one. The future society could only emerge after the overthrow of the old one by a revolution. To that end, Blanqui saw revolution as something that needed to be consciously planned, organized, and carried out through the force of arms.

Since open agitation was impossible in France during most of Blanqui's life, the only available recourse for revolutionaries was to go underground. His strategy was to organize a tightly disciplined secret society composed of virtuous revolutionaries trained in street-fighting and insurrectionary tactics. On an appointed day, this conspiracy would seize political power in Paris and, by extension, across France. Once the insurgents had power, they would create a revolutionary dictatorship that would rule on behalf of the people. This dictatorship would accomplish two things: defend the poor against the rich and educate the people in republican and socialist values. After these twin tasks were completed, the dictatorship would give way to the rule of the people and communism.

Even though Blanqui's conception of revolution was largely a technical question, the mass participation of the workers in 1848 and 1871 came about in spite of him. Blanqui misjudged the situation in prison during both those upheavals. In the end, Blanqui's efforts failed. Despite his eclectic theories, elitism, and failures, we should not simply ignore or dismiss Blanqui. He took the side of the workers in the great revolutions of the nineteenth century and warned them against trusting false friends, such as reformist socialists or neo-Jacobins. Blanqui's warnings were correct, and the moderates betrayed the cause of the working class.

Blanqui recognized that the violent seizure of power was the only way to overthrow capitalism and begin the transition to communism. Blanqui's conspiratorial strategy may have been a failure, but in treating insurrection and revolution as an art, he seriously posed the right questions that those after him, such as Lenin and Trotsky, would have to deal with: How can an insurrection be organized? What tactics are needed for an insurrection to succeed? Who are the enemies of the workers that need to be dealt with? Who should benefit from a socialist revolution? What conditions comprise a revolutionary situation? Lastly, Blanqui earned his revolutionary prestige through a lifetime of staying true to his principles despite all the suffering he endured. He remains to this very day an example of courage and commitment. For all these reasons, it is worth looking anew at the life and thoughts of Louis-Auguste Blanqui.

I. Beginnings

In the Shadow of the French Revolution

The first reference point for Blanqui's life was the impact of the struggles and ideas produced by the French Revolution of 1789. The French Revolution had changed the nature of class struggle and politics. Its experience had shown that ordinary working people could be mobilized to fight against the power of monarchs and aristocrats.

Before 1789, France was ruled by the absolute monarch, Louis XVI of the ancient Bourbon dynasty, who claimed his legitimacy to rule from the "divine right" of God. The Crown had brought France to bankruptcy through its extravagant spending on wars and chronic mismanagement. In order to improve the ancient tax system, Louis XVI convened the Estates General (parliament) in the spring of 1789 for the first time in more than a century. The king hoped to shift the burden of taxation onto the Third Estate (who constituted everyone who was not an aristocrat or member of the clergy). The Third Estate refused to obey the king and transformed the Estates General into an independent National Assembly, pledging not to disperse until they gave France a new constitution. The Third Estate's outright defiance threatened the power of the king. This act roused in the people of Paris feelings of hope that a new era was about to begin that would sweep away age-old injustices. In July, Louis XVI prepared to move troops into Paris to disperse the National Assembly and reassert his authority. On July 14, 1789, the people of Paris rallied to the defense of the National Assembly and stormed the Bastille, a hated symbol of absolutism, in search of arms. The intervention of the Parisian people saved the National Assembly. The fall of the Bastille marked a change in the course of the French Revolution. Until now, the revolution was just fighting between the Crown and the bourgeoisie. Now ordinary people were taking action and soon they would push events in radical directions.

A month later, peasants across the French countryside burned aristocratic manors, which emboldened the National Assembly to decree the abolition of feudalism. The Assembly did not make a clean break with the past in the countryside but decreed the peasantry still had to pay compensation to the aristocracy for their land. This compromise led to six further peasant revolts between 1789 and 1792.

In August 1789, the National Assembly also produced the Declaration of the Rights of Man and of the Citizen, inspired by philosophers of the Enlightenment and by the American Declaration of Independence of 1776. The basic principle of the Declaration was that all "men are born and remain free and equal in rights," entitled to the rights of liberty, private property, security, and resistance to oppression. All citizens were declared equal before the law and had the right to participate in legislation. While the Declaration asserted the principles of popular sovereignty as opposed to divine right, only "active citizens" could hold political rights and vote. This limited suffrage to just male property owners. Passive citizens, including the vast majority of people in France—non–property owners, women, slaves, children, and foreigners—were denied the right to vote.

The concerns of the urban population, who endured high food prices and poverty, were priorities in the National Assembly. If the people were going to defend their interests and advance their own demands, they had to organize themselves. The central force pushing the revolution forward in Paris were the *sansculottes*. The sansculottes were not a single class, but composed of a bourgeois minority—artisans, shopkeepers, merchants, and workers.[1] They organized political clubs that demanded price controls on essential goods such as bread and an expansion of democracy. The sansculottes' demands went further than the leadership of the National Assembly—led by the moderate Girondin Club—were willing to go. The popular movement found its champions in the radical club known as the Jacobins, or the Mountain, whose most outspoken leader was the charismatic lawyer Maximilien Robespierre.

As the French Revolution radicalized, the aristocrats grew fearful of losing their privileges to the "mob." Many aristocrats moved abroad, where they plotted to overthrow the revolution with the aid of foreign powers. In June 1791, Louis XVI was discovered to be in contact with foreign powers, justifying radical suspicion of the Crown. Many monarchs were watching events in France nervously, believing the revolution could threaten their thrones. In 1792, France declared war on the Hapsburg Monarchy of Austria, leading to wars with Prussia, Britain, and Spain. For nearly a quarter of a century, France remained at war with most of Europe.

The Girondins had originally championed war as a distraction from implementing radical changes in France. The revolutionary wars ended up having the opposite results. The Girondin-led war was poorly commanded and organized. After a series of defeats, France was vulnerable to invasion. Calls for new leadership began to grow. In August 1792, the sansculottes mobilized and went into action. They overthrew the king and formed the Paris Commune. The following month, the First Republic was proclaimed, and on January 21, 1793, the king was guillotined.

Differences remained in the Convention, which had replaced the National Assembly in 1792, over how to conduct the war. Robespierre and the Jacobins demanded a vigorous prosecution of the war with a centralized command structure and a planned economy. They also wanted to impose maximum prices on goods such as bread to solidify support from the sansculottes for military war effort. The Jacobins called for the institutionalization of terror to fight the internal enemies of the revolution, whom they said were colluding with foreign powers. The Girondins opposed state interference in the economy, and they were not willing to grant concessions to the sansculottes since these measures infringed on the rights of private property. In May 1793, dissatisfaction with the Girondins resulted in another popular rising in Paris that brought the Jacobins to power.

The following month, the Jacobins ratified a new constitution that granted sweeping social reforms and abolished the distinction between active and passive citizens, granting all adult men the vote. However, the Jacobins suspended implementing the constitution's provisions because of the need to employ emergency powers to conduct the war. Increasingly, power was concentrated in the Committee of Public Safety, led by Robespierre, which organized the economy and the military. The Committee of Public Safety placed a maximum price on bread and ensured its steady supply to the populace—thereby fulfilling Jacobin promises to the sansculottes. In the countryside, the old regime was finally swept away when feudal property titles were abolished without compensation.

Most controversially, the Jacobins instituted the Reign of Terror, utilizing the guillotine and repression against not only suspected enemies of the revolution but also to guarantee that merchants complied with price and economic controls. The Jacobins' economic controls included enforcement of maximum limits on wages, which produced anger in the sansculottes when their incomes fell. Led by radical factions, such as the Enragés and the Hébertists, the sansculottes protested against these measures and Jacobin authoritarianism. Robespierre responded to these protests by shutting down the radical clubs and executing their leaders. These actions silenced left-wing opposition to the Jacobins but undermined their own base of support.

By the summer of 1794, the Jacobins had succeeded in winning the war. Now that the republic was safe, more conservative factions and the bourgeoisie no longer saw the need for emergency measures, Jacobin radicalism, or state intervention in the economy. They feared that continued radicalism would threaten private property. On July 27, 1794 (in the month of Thermidor, according to the revolutionary calendar), Robespierre was overthrown and the revolutionary period came to an end. The Thermidorians wanted to ensure that the bourgeoisie could at last enjoy their power and wealth without worrying about popular upheaval or the demands of Jacobin virtue. By 1795, the "Thermidorian Reaction" undid the popular and democratic conquests of the revolution.

Thermidorian rule did not bring either order or stability. A scant five years later in November 1799, the brilliant general Napoleon Bonaparte overthrew the Thermidorians and instituted a military dictatorship. In 1804, Napoleon crowned himself emperor and created a new aristocracy, beginning the First French Empire. A mere eleven years after executing King Louis XVI, France was again ruled by a monarch. However, Napoleon did not reverse all the gains of the revolution. He instituted a new set of laws known as the Napoleonic Code that protected private property. The emperor's armies marched across Europe, where they abolished feudalism and spread the revolution on their bayonets. In 1815, Napoleon was finally defeated and the Bourbon king, Louis XVIII (brother of Louis XVI) returned to power.[2] Decades of war and revolution appeared to be finally at an end.

The French Revolution promised "*liberté, égalité, fraternité,*" but in the end it had granted none and, for most people, replaced one despotism for another. The ideals of 1789 and 1793 meant vastly different things to the diverse classes who had carried out the revolution. For the bourgeoisie, the revolution should stop once a constitutional government was created to protect private property. Mobilizing ordinary people was at best a necessary evil to accomplish those goals, but this could lead to the dangerous extremes of democracy and social leveling. For the sansculottes, peasants, and workers, the revolution enabled them to articulate their own radical demands. They were not simply fighting to establish bourgeois rule, but, according to Daniel Guérin, "They were making their own revolution and their enemy was privilege and oppression, whether clerical, noble or bourgeois in form."[3] It was from the radical currents of the French Revolution that utopian socialism and modern communism were born. These ideas would not only seek to realize the promises of the French Revolution but also confront the new problems of industrial capitalism. The radicals of Blanqui's generation would inherit this legacy, and they had to answer the following questions: What should future revolutions do differently? How would they move beyond the limits of 1789 and 1793?

The Blanquis

For Jean Dominique Blanqui, the French Revolution brought both anguish and social advance.[4] He was born in 1757 in Nice, then ruled by the Duke of Savoy. Jean Dominique's family was enlightened and middle class, sharing the bourgeois outlook of the revolution. In 1792, when Nice was conquered by France, Jean Dominique was catapulted into politics and elected to the Convention. Not a very adept politician, he allied with the Girondins as their popularity was evaporating. In October of 1793, Jean Dominique's Girondin sympathies led to his arrest and imprisonment by the Jacobins. When Robespierre was overthrown, Jean Dominique was released. He welcomed the conservative climate of the Thermidorian Reaction.

In 1797, Jean Dominique married his landlady's niece, the seventeen-year-old Sophie Brionville, who would bear him ten children. Sophie had a strong, independent character and frame of mind. While Jean Dominique was imprisoned, she smuggled him news and letters. Sophie risked being branded an enemy of the revolution for being loyal to her future husband.

Despite his rising social status, Jean Dominique never adjusted to Parisian politics. To escape Paris, he took the growing family back to Nice. Jean Dominique welcomed Napoleon's rise to power, believing Bonaparte represented stability in contrast to the "twin extremes" of royalism and Jacobinism. After 1799, Jean Dominique's loyalty to Napoleon was rewarded when he was appointed sub-prefect of nearby Puget-Théniers. The Blanqui family passed the years of the First Empire enjoying their newfound social status and wealth in Puget-Théniers. While there, Sophie gave birth to a son, Louis-Auguste on February 1, 1805.

The young Auguste grew up nurtured by the powerful hand of his father. Jean Dominique taught his son to revere both the emperor and the tricolor flag. Auguste learned to love France and its achievements as the pinnacle of enlightenment and civilization. After the fall of Napoleon in 1815, Auguste's nationalism was reinforced after witnessing Prussian troops march into Puget-Théniers and threaten his mother. Years later, writing in the third person, he recalled the military occupation as the start of his "declaration of war upon all factions that represent the past [...]. The spectacle of the acts of violence [against the local population] had a profound effect on him, and decided the course of his whole life." [5]

Due to his Girondin and Napoleonic past, Jean Dominique was dismissed by the Bourbons, reversing the family's fortunes. The Blanquis were saved from destitution when Sophie inherited an estate— the chateau de Grand Mont in Aunay-sous-Auneau. After Sophie carelessly indulged in shopping for jewelry in the shops of Paris, the Blanquis nearly lost their second chance.

In 1818, the elder Blanqui son, Jérôme-Adolphe, who was working as a tutor in Paris, sent for Auguste and a younger sister to live with him. Auguste enrolled as a student at the Institution Massin, excelling in Latin, history, math, and geography.

During these years, Auguste and Jérôme-Adolphe were practically inseparable. The elder brother took Auguste on tours of Paris, where he learned to love its people, streets, monuments, and history. This knowledge of Paris would serve Auguste well when determining where to place barricades. Jérôme-Adolphe was impressed with his brother's achievements. He wrote in a letter to their father: "One day this child will astonish the world!"[6] The two brothers were destined to travel widely divergent paths. Auguste would become a feared communist revolutionary, while Jérôme-Adolphe became a famous liberal economist.

After Auguste graduated with honors from Institution Massin, he continued his education at Lycée Charlemagne, studying law and medicine. While many of Auguste's classmates were aristocratic and quite well off, he was forced to work as a private tutor to support himself. Here, Auguste first encountered economics, through the liberal Jean-Baptiste Say. Say was an advocate for laissez-faire, competition, and free trade, and an opponent of popular uprisings, the Bourbons, and Bonaparte. Auguste's impression of Say was not a positive one.

Later, he judged Say's ideas as immoral and promoting "a code of mutual extermination."[7] Ironically, Jérôme-Adolphe became a disciple of Say and succeeded him as chair of political economy at the Conservatoire National des Arts et Métiers in 1833.

Auguste was not totally absorbed in his studies and confessed later that he was interested in "any rumor of polemics" or political discussions at the Lycée.[8] Beyond these hints, there was little indication of his future career as a street fighter and professional revolutionary. Auguste appeared to be destined for a stellar career as a doctor or a lawyer.

II. COMMITMENT

THE RESTORATION

The Bourbon Restoration of 1815 did not mean that all the gains of the French Revolution were simply erased. The land titles of the aristocracy were not restored. To ease the return of the monarchy, King Louis XVIII granted a constitution and created a representative body, the Chamber of Deputies. However, the Chamber's powers were limited. The high-property qualification for voting was meant to reserve high government positions for the nobility while excluding the bourgeoisie. The bourgeoisie lived uneasily under the Restoration. The revolution of 1789 had given them power and the opportunities to expand their wealth. Now, the aristocrats returning from exile yearned to forget the past quarter century and recreate the old world that the revolution had taken away. Duvergier de Hauranne described the chasm that separated the two classes as "two peoples separated by different memories, ideas and habits, and who were no longer able to understand one another. They were two armies which had fought one against the other: what one celebrated as victories the other deplored as defeats."[1]

In 1815, the royalist-led Chamber organized the White Terror that targeted the beneficiaries of the revolution, especially former

Jacobins and Bonapartists. The White Terror purged close to a third of the government and sent thousands more to prison.[2]

The royalist repression meant that opposition was effectively silenced and unable to demand even the slightest concessions. With legal avenues of redress closed, plots, riots, rebellion, and conspiracy proliferated. To eradicate all opposition, Louis XVIII created a Ministry of the Interior to spy on real and imagined opponents of the Bourbons and maintain public order.

By the early 1820s, illegal opposition coalesced in the Carbonari movement. The Carbonari, inspired by a liberal movement in Italy of the same name, was a national movement centered in Paris. The group was united only by their hatred of the Bourbons.[3] Due to their lack of a positive program, the Carbonari attracted many diverse groups such as liberals, Bonapartists, Orleanists, radicals, republicans, students, elements of the middle class, and most importantly officers and soldiers, both retired and on active service. These Bonapartist veterans of Napoleon's Grand Armée provided the military and cadre leadership of the Carbonari. There was little to no working-class involvement in the Carbonari.[4] The Carbonari's agents were organized in a network of cells and had 50,000 members in 1822.[5] Despite its impressive size, the Carbonari's structure made it difficult to communicate and coordinate actions.

In late 1821 and early 1822, the Carbonari launched a series of failed insurrections and putsches in Saumur, Belfort, Toulon, Nantes, La Rochelle, Strasbourg, and Paris.[6] The Bourbons cracked down, arrested Carbonari organizers, and placed them on trial. Despite their failures, the rebels had struck a chord with the people. When four Carbonari sergeants from La Rochelle—Jean-François Bories, Jean-Joseph Pommier, Charles Goubin, and Marius-Claude Raoulx—were sentenced to die, there were calls for mercy.[7] Louis XVIII and his advisers were determined to set an example.[8] On September 21, 1822, the four were guillotined at the Place de Grève in Paris. Legend has it that their last words were the cry of "Vive la Liberté!"[9] Among the witnesses to their execution was the seventeen-year-old Auguste Blanqui. His lifelong commitment to the revolutionary cause can be traced to the execution of these "martyrs to Liberty."[10]

Upon Blanqui's graduation from the Lycée Charlemagne in 1824, he joined the Carbonari. He did not stay in the Carbonari for long, since the organization was fracturing under the double impact of internal splits and state repression. The Carbonari had been dependent on avoiding discussions on the shape of a post-Bourbon France. When differences invariably arose among the members about their goals, it resulted in the organization splitting into rival factions with each claiming to be the "legitimate" Carbonari movement and denouncing the others. Over the next several years, three congresses were held to mend the splits and unite the movement. These unification congresses failed, and the Carbonari were left divided and moribund.[11]

THE CONSPIRATORIAL TRADITION

The brief sojourn in the Carbonari left a lasting mark on Blanqui. According to his biographer Gustave Geffroy, "Blanqui, introduced to politics under the Restoration, assumed the habits of a conspirator of the Restoration period, and the Carbonarist cell became for him the ideal type of secret society and of all possible political organization."[12] Future Blanquist organizations would all be organized similarly to the Carbonari, containing a top-down structure with cells at the base isolated from one another and the leadership. Only one member of a cell would be in contact with a single superior above them in the organizational chain. The leadership would be known only to a few trusted members in order to prevent their arrest. The Carbonari's organizational structure was elitist and hierarchical by design. For Blanqui, this type of organization was the only realistic way for revolutionaries to practically organize opposition against the Bourbons, and, later, the July Monarchy, and the Second Empire.[13]

In the 1820s, Blanqui, analogous to the Carbonari, had no plans for what happened after overthrowing the Bourbons. His ideas remained vague and underdeveloped. Due to his upbringing, he had a reverence for Napoleon that he shared with many of the Carbonari's cadre. While in the Carbonari, he was exposed to other ideas as well—such as republicanism and liberalism. These Carbonari republicans kept alive memories of 1793 and the First Republic, which would later have a profound impact on Auguste.

Following Auguste's graduation in 1824, Jérôme-Adolphe helped him obtain a job as a journalist for the *Courier Français* and the *Journal de Commerce*. He did not last long for either paper, since his pay was low and he wanted more secure employment. To that end, he accepted a job as a tutor for the family of Jean Dominique Compans, a general and veteran of the Napoleonic Wars, at the château de Blagnac, in the Garonne.

From 1824 to 1826, Blanqui not only worked as a tutor but carefully prepared himself for a revolutionary life. He read extensively and assumed a spartan lifestyle—he abstained from alcohol and maintained a strictly vegetarian diet. Blanqui kept his bedroom window open at all times and learned to inure himself against the cold.[14] This strict regimen would serve him well during the long years in prison.

CHARLES X

Despite the White Terror, Louis XVIII had made some half-hearted efforts to reach an accommodation with the bourgeoisie and the legacy of the French Revolution. This changed after his brother, Charles X, ascended to the throne in 1824. The new king was determined to roll back any trace of the revolution and return to the values of the Ancien Régime. Charles X intended to compensate the émigrés whose landed property was confiscated by the revolution and restore the Catholic Church's powers in order to bolster a renewed divine monarchy.[15] Despite Charles X's reactionary plans, at the beginning of his reign there was little organized opposition.

When Blanqui returned to Paris in 1826 to study law and medicine at the Sorbonne, monarchist reaction was at its peak. Then on November 19, 1827, the liberals won elections to the Chamber of Deputies. There were celebrations in Paris, leading to clashes between students and the army. Blanqui took part in the street fighting, and at rue Saint-Denis, he was wounded three times. One wound was a bullet that pierced his neck and was nearly fatal. Thanks to his mother's care, Blanqui fully recovered by the beginning of 1828.[16]

Years later, Blanqui recalled the street fighting of 1827 as the moment when he "rediscovered the people of the first Revolution, with their heroic rags, their bare arms, their improvised weapons, their indomitable courage and their irresistible anger."[17] This was a change in his politics from Bonapartism to Jacobinism. Blanqui became "a confessed republican and revolutionary."[18] He began to see power residing in ordinary people taking to the streets to challenge the status quo. The lesson was not lost on Blanqui that if the people wanted to succeed, then they needed organized and determined leadership who would stand with the crowd. He carefully noted that the people had failed in 1827 because they were "abandoned by the liberal leaders."[19] Every revolution of Blanqui's life would prove to him that the liberals would either compromise with reaction or leave the field of battle before victory was won, ultimately betraying the people.[20]

Amélie-Suzanne

While attending the Sorbonne, Blanqui supplemented his income by working as a tutor at a boarding school. One of his students was a young girl and a talented artist named Amélie-Suzanne Serre, with whom he fell in love. Amélie-Suzanne shared Blanqui's affections. She came from a conservative and conventional middle-class family who disapproved of the young radical. During their nine years of courtship, the consequences of Blanqui's revolutionary activism became clear to Amélie-Suzanne: police harassment, street fighting, and long prison terms. This did not dissuade Amélie-Suzanne, who married Blanqui in August 1834. The couple had two children: Estève (1834–1884), nicknamed Romeo, and a second son, who was born in 1835 but died in childbirth. The years of marriage and family would be the happiest of Blanqui's life.[21]

The Atheist Crusade

After recovering from the wounds he received in 1827, Blanqui spent his first time in jail. He was arrested while visiting his father's hometown of Nice but was quickly released. Afterward, Blanqui took a short trip to Spain, where he reacted with disgust at the pervasive influence of the Catholic Church. Throughout his life, Blanqui would be fiercely anti-clerical. For him, the Catholic Church was one of the bulwarks of reaction and an enemy of all forms of revolution, republicanism, and socialism. Blanqui wrote years later: "The priests' teachings means darkness and oppression. The black army, with a hundred thousand male and female soldiers, goes full of fury, spreading darkness and extinguishing enlightenment everywhere."[22]

In order to overcome religion, Blanqui believed that it was necessary to make education universal, so that people would be enlightened. Once the people were educated, then they would cast aside their religious superstition. Blanqui said, "The experiment of the centuries shows that the only agent of progress is education, that the light spouts (almost) only out of the exchange (and the shock) of human thought, that consequently all that supports and multiplies this exchange is to the good, all that removes it or obstructs it is evil."[23] The importance of atheism and the role of education would remain two of the central planks of Blanqui's political thinking.

Blanqui's atheism rested upon the foundation of materialism. For Blanqui, materialism (or naturalism), "restores [human] dignity, activity and independence."[24] While religion served the wealthy classes, materialism "served the masses in their struggle against the bourgeoisie."[25] By this logic, materialism had given birth to science and human initiative, while religion and spirituality brought forth superstition, ignorance, and fatalism. This meant that religion was the natural ally and bulwark of the state since it kept the people ignorant. At one point, Blanqui said, "God is the means of government, a protector of the privileged against the multitude. The proletariat . . . should distrust any emblem which does not bear in bold letters the motto: Atheism and materialism."[26] To Blanqui, every assault on religion, whether from materialism, atheism, or secular education, was to be celebrated since they challenged ignorance and furthered the revolutionary cause.

Religion was harmful not only to society, but to any revolutionary movement that embraced it. In later years, he viewed with scorn the independence movements of Poland, Italy, and Ireland because of their religious coloration.

Even though the focus of Blanqui's hatred was the Catholic Church, he spared no religion from criticism: "All forms of theism— Judaism, Christianity and Islamism—must be annihilated. This is our guiding principle, the fixed point of our compass."[27] He attacked Judaism not just on religious grounds but also for its supposed economic role through usury. In some of his notes, Blanqui veered into anti-Semitism and identified the Jews as capitalists personified. He said the Jews are "the type, the ideal and the incarnation of swindling, usury and rapacity. They are the horror of the nations because of their pitiless cupidity, as they had once been because of their hostility and war to the death against the human race."[28]

THE UTOPIANS

Returning to Paris in 1829, Blanqui gave up his studies in law and took a job as a stenographer for the moderate opposition paper, *Le Globe*. The paper was noted for its liberal reputation, and its contributors included Victor Cousin, Augustin Therry, Sainte-Beauve, François Chateaubriand, André Ampère, and a young Victor Hugo. Blanqui bitterly described *Le Globe's* liberal ideas as "sacrosanct dogmas, taken out of the gospel according to St. Malthus, St. Ricardo, St. Jeremy Bentham and other learned professors of usury and selfishness."[29]

Only one member of *Le Globe* earned Blanqui's praise—Pierre Leroux. He was a former member of the Carbonari[30] and one of the popularizers, if not the originator, of the term *communism*. To Leroux, the name of communism "designate[d] a republic in which equality would hold sway."[31] Leroux was also an adherent of the utopian socialist school of Saint-Simonism.[32]

While Blanqui was impressed with Leroux, he found his utopian socialist ideas far less attractive. As mentioned earlier, the utopians picked up where 1789 had left off. While the French Revolution had ended special privileges according to birth and social status by making people equal before the law, the utopians believed that formal equality did not go far enough. They argued that private property was the root cause of inequality. The most prominent utopian socialists in the early nineteenth century were Saint-Simon (1760–1825), Charles Fourier (1772–1837), and Robert Owen (1771–1858). Though they differed markedly in their backgrounds and temperaments, all the major utopian thinkers were fierce critics of capitalism, children of the Enlightenment, and convinced of the power to reason to solve any problem. To that end, they constructed detailed blueprints to remake society without classes and inequality. By the 1830s, the utopians had gained popularity in the emerging French working-class communities.

The utopians eschewed politics and revolution, believing it was necessary to appeal to men of good will—such as technicians, philanthropists, and even the nobility and kings—in order to redress class conflict. The utopians recognized the existence of class struggle, but they conceived of class relations not as one of conflict but of harmony. According to their conception, human history advanced rationally. In time, the upper classes would accept the dictates of "reason" and collaborate with the workers to end class conflict and create a new society.

Blanqui held these utopian plans for constructing a future socialism in contempt. According to him, it was impossible to envision the future until the past was swept away. That the utopians said otherwise was proof that they were prisoners of dogmatic thinking akin to religion:

> No! No one has access to the secret of the future. Scarcely possible for even the most clairvoyant are certain presentiments, rapid glimpses, a vague and fugitive coup d'oeil. The Revolution alone will reveal the horizon, will gradually remove the veils and up the roads, or rather the multiple paths that lead to the new order. Those who pretend to have in their pocket a complete map of this unknown land—they truly are the madmen.[33]

Blanqui said the essential task of socialists was political action and organizing for revolution, not laying out plans for a future society:

One of our most grotesque presumptions is that we barbarians, we ignoramuses, pose as legislatures of future generations. Those generations, for which we take the trouble to feel concern and prepare the foundations, will render us a hundred times more pity than the caveman inspires in us, and their compassion will be a great deal more reasonable than ours.[34]

Socialists and communists needed to be grounded in the reality of the class struggle. They could not be concerned with what came after the revolution: "Let us take care of today. Tomorrow does not belong to us. Our only duty is to prepare the good materials for building that tomorrow, the rest is beyond our competence. . . . Communism, which is the revolution itself, must be wary of the allures of utopia and never separate itself from politics.[35]

To Blanqui, the most detailed and perfect utopia was just a dream. It made no sense to simply imagine a better future without creating the means to achieve it.

Blanqui's hostility to the utopians was not total. He could see a basis for unity with them in current political struggles, provided that speculations about the future were left aside. His attitude toward Proudhonism can be extended to include other utopians: "Communism and Proudhonism argue vigorously on the bank of a river over whether there is a field of corn or wheat on the other side. Let us cross first, we will see when get there."[36]

It did not matter if socialists had not worked out plans for the future. What mattered was exposing the injustices of the existing society and organizing to destroy it.

The utopians were responding to the defenders of capitalism, who demanded that socialists must have a complete plan for a new society. Blanqui thought this utopian concern was irrelevant. He knew that the capitalist concern for blueprints merely shielded their own self-interest. As he said: "It is an amusing thing, when one discusses communism, how the adversary's terrors instinctively bring them to this inevitable piece of furniture! 'Who will empty the chamber pot?' It is always the first cry. 'Who will empty my chamber pot?' they really mean to say."[37]

Despite Blanqui's major differences with utopian theories like Saint-Simonism, his own socialism did adopt their understanding of *association*. The origins of association lay in the earliest forms of human cooperation to counteract individualism. Blanqui viewed individualism as antithetical to the interests of society, since the motivation for development came at the expense of others. In a society founded on individualism, others with individualistic drives would frustrate social advance and reduce people to the state of animals. Association would protect the weak, encourage solidarity, and prevent the mutual self-destruction inherent in individualism. Progress could be measured with increasing association and the weakening of individualism: "Equality, therefore, should only be realized through a regime of association, substituted in place of the reign of individual property. This is why we see all the men of the future working fervently to clarify the elements of this association. We expect to make our contribution to this labour of devotion at a later date."[38]

For Blanqui, the highest stage of association was communism, which was the final triumph of both universal enlightenment and association over ignorance and individualism.

Toward July

While at *Le Globe*, Blanqui reported on parliamentary proceedings and followed the escalating political situation. By 1830, the Chamber of Deputies was openly opposed to the king. The elections of June 1830 brought a sweeping liberal victory. That same month, Charles X embarked on a relatively easy conquest of Algiers, and it was feared by the opposition that he would assume dictatorial powers granted to him by Article 14 of the Charter."[39] The worst fears of the opposition were realized on July 26, 1830, when the king passed four ordinances that curtailed freedom of the press, excluded even the big bourgeoisie from voting, and called for new rigged elections.[40] If these ordinances went unchallenged, the monarchy would have the type of power they hadn't known since 1789.

On the eve of the July Revolution, Blanqui described the opposition deputies as "revolutionists, but they did not know it."[41] When Charles X issued his four ordinances, Blanqui predicted the outcome of the crisis to his terrified and cowardly colleagues: "Before the week is over, it will all be settled by rifle shots."[42] *Le Globe* staff disbelieved Blanqui, but within hours barricades would rise across Paris in what would be called the Three Glorious Days.

During the July Revolution, Parisian workers armed themselves with pikes and whatever guns they could get a hold of. Blanqui urged his colleagues at *Le Globe* to take the side of the workers and lead the revolutionary movement. This was too much for them. They were scared enough to step outside the law but feared the armed workers more than the Bourbons.[43] Despite the hopes of *Le Globe* members for a peaceful settlement, Blanqui made his choice: "For my part . . . I'll take a gun and a cockade."[44] For the next three days, Blanqui found himself in the thick of the revolution. He took a leading role in the streets. Blanqui's courage during the July Revolution was recognized by the new government who awarded him The Declaration of July. This would be the only official decoration that Blanqui would ever be awarded by the French state.[45]

While the fighting was going on, Blanqui issued two proclamations. The one read

Call to Arms

Art 1 – All citizens from 16 to 50 years of age are called upon for the defense of the fatherland and of freedom.

Art 2 – Men between 16 and 30 years of age, armed or unarmed, are to report to the Place de l'Hôtel de Ville in order to be organized in battalions.

Art 3 – Men between 30 and 50 shall remain in their neighborhoods in order to prepare resistance there.

Art 4 – Barricades shall be constructed every 50 meters on all streets. The stones should be removed and on the principal streets the stones should be taken to the upper floors in order to be thrown at the troops of Charles X.

Art 5 – Former military men, officers, non-commissioned officers and soldiers are called to the Hotel de Ville in order to form the cadres of the popular battalions.

Art 6 – Commissions will be established for: 1 – provisioning, 2 – armament, 3 – supplying of ammunition. Citizens capable of fulfilling these functions are asked to present themselves to the Hotel de Ville.

Art 7 – Armorers shall deliver firearms, powder and bullets found in their stores to the people. The state will reimburse them for the price of these objects with a 25% bonus for the risks involved.[46]

Blanqui wrote a second address as a counter to the right-wing opposition to the Bourbons. The right wing feared the July insurgents and wanted a quick compromise with Charles X. To stop this, the liberals and republicans looked to General Lafayette, the seventy-three-year-old progressive general and symbol of the French and American Revolutions. To preempt any compromise with the king, they advocated for Lafayette to impose a dictatorship.

In his second address, Blanqui supported a potential Lafayette dictatorship but said the revolution would not compromise with forces of the old order. Instead, Blanqui's address argued that with Lafayette's support, a republic would be created to protect the people's rights and grant them equality.[47] Blanqui's two declarations showed that several parts of his political thinking had come together: the people could only be victorious if they possessed a disciplined organization with a revolutionary leadership.

When the July Revolution was over, Charles X fled France. Lafayette and the liberals did not establish a republic but crowned Louis-Philippe of the House of Orleans as the "Citizen King." While it can be readily argued that the insurgents of July were not republicans, the radical opposition felt betrayed.[48] Blanqui lamented a few years later:

By what fatality did that revolution made by the people alone, and that should have marked the end of the exclusive reign of the bourgeoisie as well as the success of popular interests and might, have no other results than the establishing of the despotism of the middle class, aggravating the poverty of the workers and peasants, and plunging France a bit further into the mud? Alas, the people, like the other old man, knew how to win, but not how to profit from its victory. The fault is not all their own.[49]

Blanqui was determined that in the next round of struggle not only would the people win but also that they alone would profit from their victory.

III. The Underground

The July Monarchy

The Bourbon Restoration was based upon the supremacy of the landlords, who grudgingly, if at all, were willing to share power with the bourgeoisie; by contrast, the July Monarchy was the rule of the bankers. As Marx wrote in "The Class Struggles in France": "After the July Revolution, when the liberal banker Laffitte led his compère, the Duke of Orléans, in triumph to the Hôtel de Ville, he let fall the words: 'From now on the bankers will rule.' Laffitte had betrayed the secret of the revolution."[1] It was not without reason that the July Monarchy was called the bourgeois monarchy. The July Monarchy made a few cosmetic changes and concessions: suffrage was expanded from 100,000 to 240,000 votes. Still, due to high property qualifications, most of France's adult male population of 9,000,000 was excluded from voting.

Marx bitterly described the July Monarchy as

> nothing but a joint-stock company for the exploitation of France's national wealth, the dividends of which were divided among ministers, Chambers, 240,000 voters and their adherents. Louis Philippe was the director of this company—Robert Macaire on the throne. Trade, industry, agriculture, shipping, the interests of the industrial bourgeoisie, were bound to be continually endangered and prejudiced under this system. Cheap government, gouvernement á bon marché was what it had inscribed in the July days on its banner.[2]

25

For the bourgeoisie, the July Revolution was their ideal revolution. They created a constitutional monarchy that protected their wealth without resorting to any of the excesses of Jacobinism. Marx said:

> Finally, in 1830 the bourgeoisie put into effect its wishes of the year 1789, with the only difference that its political enlightenment was now completed, that it no longer considered the constitutional representative state as a means for achieving the ideal of the state, the welfare of the world and universal human aims but, on the contrary, had acknowledged it as the official expression of its own exclusive power and the political recognition of its own special interests.[3]

NEMESIS

The workers who fought and died on the Parisian barricades had hoped for an alleviation to their suffering and representation in government, not simply a change of dynasties. An economic crisis that began in 1827 caused food to grow scarce and the cost of living to rise. Even with the fall of the Bourbons, the crisis continued unabated.[4] The efforts of workers to organize were met with arrests and prison. Soon, many workers were willing to take up arms once again.

By the end of 1830, Blanqui was openly opposed to the July Monarchy. As Bernstein observed, he became an activist and proved an apt learner in agitation and propaganda:

> facts imprinted themselves on his mind with the effect of a seal; and he had the faculty of distilling from them the active principles that governed his conduct. . . . At the Sorbonne and Law School he cornered students with arguments, exhorting them to follow him to higher ground from which they could take a critical view of the recently established regime.[5]

The first results of Blanqui's activism was a student meeting he organized to pay final respects to the liberal writer Benjamin Constant, who had died on December 8, 1830. At first sight, Blanqui taking the lead in organizing this gathering may appear strange since Constant's politics were far removed from his. Constant was an advocate for individual liberty, a decentralized government, and a limited monarchy.[6] Despite this, Constant was popular among students and had supported the July Revolution. Blanqui saw his funeral as an opportunity to mobilize the students. As he said in his initial organizing call:

> Benjamin Constant made it a point of pride to be the friend of young people. Until his last moment, he raised his voice to defend us, because the youth of France, just as much as freedom, needed to be defended, even after the battle of the July Days. Five days before his death, the assembly halls still resounded to his patriotic tones; he died in battle as a combatant for the principles and the achievements of our revolution. An entire people will accompany the mortal remains of the defender of our rights to his last resting place.[7]

Blanqui ended his address by calling on mourners, both armed and unarmed, to meet at the place du Pantheon to honor Constant on December 30, 1830. There was no fighting that day, but the workers and students did march together.[8]

The following month, Blanqui wrote an address for a student association named the Committee of Schools, where he condemned the government for breaking its promises and not granting freedom to the people. He told the audience:

> We admit that our hearts have withered at the sight of so many broken promises. Our good faith, the faith of simple and trusting young people, has been outrageously betrayed, our future has been sacrificed, and the blood of our brothers appears to count for nothing. But it is easier to deceive us than to demoralize us, and since the powerful only hear when you speak loudly, we will make ourselves heard. We have been taught an excellent lesson, and learned that when it comes to freedom, you cannot wait for it; you must take it. As the elderly like to say, experience is good for the young.
>
> Students, young people, have the right to join together in order to guide their efforts towards a common goal, and they will use this right. As for their goal, it is simple: for them it is a matter of ensuring that the July revolution is not a lie; every edifice built by the Empire and the Restoration must be overthrown, and since not one single stone of this edifice is yet to fall, they will work indefatigably to demolish and destroy it.
>
> ...
>
> Through persecution and violence we will march firmly,

unshakably, towards our goal. We are young, we are patient; we will not easily give up on freedom. We won it in July, and by January it was already lost. Well! It is worth being won twice. Legitimate right and the future are ours; the day of justice will arrive.

And all of you, our friends and brothers, students of the schools of Paris and the whole of France, join your efforts with ours. Our isolated cries would get lost in the immense tumult of society; but united as a solid mass of acclamation they will form one great voice that will silence these charmers of tyranny. Let us rally around the immortal motto: freedom! In the hubbub of all the cries that the passions and base interests have sought and still seek to mix with this sacred cry: freedom! Its echo alone stirs our hearts; it alone has a right to our love, our devotion: we want it, and we will have it.[9]

Blanqui's speech was a barely concealed call to insurrection that frightened the monarchy, leading to his arrest and three weeks of imprisonment.

FRIENDS OF THE PEOPLE

The development of industrial capitalism during the July Monarchy brought with it major changes in the methods of labor and workers' conditions. For one, industrialization led to the growth of unplanned cities without the most elemental forms of sanitation. There were outbreaks of epidemics such as cholera that ravaged Paris in 1831 (claiming the life of Blanqui's father). Secondly, traditional handicraft, artisan, and independent forms of labor were slowly being eroded and replaced by factory labor. More and more artisans, journeymen, and others were finding themselves transformed into wage workers with low pay and unsafe working conditions. By 1848, out of a population of 36 million, 14 million were agricultural workers, while the number of urban workers was more than 5 million. Of these 5 million, around 1 million were industrial workers, employed in small workshops or factories averaging ten workers per factory.[10] Slowly France was becoming more capitalist, even though agriculture and small industry predominated in the economy.

The artisan-workers resisted the encroachments of this new order. Their vision of a just society was influenced by the experience of the French Revolution and Jacobinism. According to the historian Wolfgang Abendroth,

> The French Revolution succeeded in establishing important premises for the future development of the European working class: an awareness of the necessity for both political democracy and international solidarity in the struggle for human rights. The experience of social conflict against the bourgeoisie had led to serious consideration of how society could be transformed, and this had its effect on small groups of workers in both England and France. For such people capitalist ownership of the means of production was no longer an unquestioned or sacrosanct principle of economic life.[11]

The workers remembered the Jacobins for punishing aristocrats and ensuring that the poor could eat. Now workers saw themselves standing against the capitalists, who acted as aristocrats in the factories.[12] In 1831, a writer for the *Journal des Débats* declared, "Every manufacturer lives in his factory like a plantation owner among his slaves."[13]

An excerpt from a working-class Jacobin publication of the 1830s showed its use of revolutionary language to express the new class divide between workers and capitalists:

> The most numerous and most useful class of society is, without contradiction, the class of workers. Without capital it has no value; without it no machines, no industry, no commerce. . . . But we are no longer in a time where workers are serfs that a master could sell or kill with ease; we are no longer in that distant epoch where our class counted in society only as the arm of the social body. . . . Our industry, which you have exploited for so long, belongs to us as our own, and the enlightenment of instruction, the blood that we have spilled for liberty has given us the means and the right to free ourselves forever from the servitude in which you hold us.[14]

To the workers in the urban factories, enduring their wretched conditions, it was becoming very clear who their enemies were. The Lyon workers' uprisings of 1831 and 1834[15] showed that they were willing to resist their oppressors, just as their ancestors had in 1789.

Blanqui was growing aware of this growing class divide. Already an adherent to the Jacobin tradition, he would renew and radicalize republicanism by orienting it to the working class.

When he was released from prison in February 1831, Blanqui returned to political activity and joined the Parisian republican group, Society of the Friends of the People, who had between 400 and 600 members. The Friends of the People was formed on July 30, 1830, shortly after the revolution, to continue agitation for a republic, but it was quickly outmaneuvered by both the Orleanists and the conservatives. With a republic denied them, the Friends of the People decided to focus on defending basic civil liberties such as freedom of assembly and the press. The Friends began moving leftward and rejected economic liberalism, due to the involvement of Blanqui and other radicals such as Charles Teste (a friend and student of Philippe Buonarroti), and ex-Carbonari Ulysse Trélat.[16]

The growing radicalism and popularity of the Friends brought the group to the attention of the police. In July 1831, Blanqui was one of fifteen members of the Friends who were arrested on charges of treason and for violating laws censoring the press. The government dropped the charge of treason, but Blanqui and the others were still placed on trial for violating the restrictive press laws.[17]

When Blanqui and the others were brought to trial in January of 1832, he was asked by the judge to give his profession.

> Presiding judge: What is your profession?
> Blanqui: Proletarian.
> Judge: That is not a profession.
> Blanqui: What! Not a profession? It is the profession of thirty million Frenchmen who live by their labour and who are deprived of political rights.
> Judge: Well, so be it. Let the clerk record that the accused is a proletarian.[18]

The speech itself was a condemnation of the July Monarchy and a call to arms. Blanqui began, "I am accused of having told thirty million French people, proletarians like me, that they had the right to live."[19] Blanqui also rejected the right of the Orleanist court to try him by stating: "I am thus not in standing before judges, but am in the presence of enemies. As a result, there would be no point in defending myself."[20] Rather than defend himself from the charges, he took it upon himself to condemn the existing social order:

> As for our role, it is written in advance; the role of accuser is the only one which is appropriate for the oppressed.
>
> The public prosecutor has, so to speak, conjured up in your minds a slave revolt in order to stir up your hatred through fear: "You see," he says, "this is the war of the poor against the rich; all those who have property have an interest in repelling the invasion. We bring your enemies before you. Strike them now, before they become any more fearsome![21]
>
> *Yes, Messrs, this is the war between the rich and the poor: the rich wanted it thus, because they are the aggressors.*[22]

Of the ruling classes, he said, "*As for the privileged few, who live off the backs of the proletariat,* they are the legal owners who are threatened with pillaging from a greedy rabble. This is not the first time that executioners act as if they are the victims. . . . The present government has no base other than this iniquitous distribution of benefits and burdens."[23]

Blanqui argued that the July Revolution betrayed the hopes of the working class and asked the court:

> Did the proletariat then fight simply to change the face on the banknotes they so seldom see? Are we that curious about new medals that we overturned thrones in order to give free rein to this whimsicality?
>
> This is the opinion of a ministerial propagandist who claims that in July we *continued to* want a constitutional monarchy, with Louis-Philippe taking the place of Charles X. The people, according to him, fought only as an instrument of the middle classes; that is to say that the proletarians are gladiators who kill and are killed for the amusement and benefit of the privileged few, who applaud from their balconies....once the battle has ended, of course.[24]

According to Blanqui, the workers had fought for something different in July. They had wanted a republic that would guarantee "*Freedom! Well-Being! Dignity abroad!*"[25]

Instead of a republic, the workers found that the new regime changed little for the better and that their protests were met with prison. Blanqui eloquently summed up how workers felt about the transition from the Bourbon to Orleanist dynasty as follows:

> Glorious workers, whose dying hand I grasped in a final farewell on the battlefield, whose dying faces I covered with rags, you died happy in the midst of a victory which should have redeemed your race. And yet, six months later, I found your children in the deepest dungeons, and each evening I fell asleep on my pallet to the sound of their moaning, to the imprecations of their torturers, and to the whistle of the whip that silenced their cries.[26]

However, the message of Blanqui's defense speech was not one of hopelessness. Even though the workers had been robbed of a republic in the July Revolution, he warned the government:

> You confiscated the rifles of July. Yes, but the bullets have been fired. Every bullet of the Parisian workers is making its way around the world. They strike without cease, and they will continue to strike until not a single enemy of freedom and the happiness of the people is left standing.[27]

According to Blanqui, the Lyon uprising of November 1831 proved that workers would continue fighting for their own interests:

> The whole country was moved by pity at the sight of this army of ghosts, half consumed by hunger, running into the grapeshot so that at least they could die instantly.
> And it is not only in Lyon; workers are dying everywhere, crushed by taxes. These men, once so proud of a victory that linked their arrival on the political stage to the triumph of freedom, whose revival required all of Europe, are fighting hunger that does not leave them enough strength to protest. [28]

To Blanqui, the existing order did not represent the working class: "The proletarian remains on the outside. The Chamber, elected by the monopolisers of power, continue unperturbed, manufacturing tax, penal and administrative laws, all with the same aim of exploitation."[29] Blanqui denied that workers under the Orleanist Monarchy could achieve any meaningful redress through peaceful reforms:

> The organs of the ministries smugly repeat that avenues are available for proletarians to voice their grievances; that the law provides them with the regular means through which to advance their interests. This is an insult. . . . The laws are made by a hundred thousand voters, applied by a hundred thousand jurors, enforced by a hundred

thousand urban national guards, for the rural national guard, which too closely resembles the people has been disorganized with great care, And these voters, these jurors, these national guardsmen are the same individuals, those who accumulate the most conflicting roles and are once legislators, judges and soldiers, such that the same man who in the morning created a deputy, that is, the law, applies this law at midday in his capacity as a juror, and carries it out in the evening in the streets while wearing the national guard uniform. What are the thirty million proletarians doing while all these changes occur? They pay.[30]

Most of the defense speech was a condemnation of the July Monarchy, but Blanqui said it was his duty and those with a sense of social justice

> to call on the masses to smash the yoke of misery and ignominy I have carried out this duty and, regardless of imprisonment, we will carry it out until the bitter end by defying our enemies. When you have behind you a great mass of people marching towards the triumph of its well-being and freedom, you must know how to throw yourself into the ditch in order to act as a fascine and fill it in and build a road for them.[31]

Blanqui's bravado and fiery indictment of the existing order brought him a year in prison for insulting the court (he was acquitted of the press-related charge). The speech marked him out as an important and charismatic figure on the radical left. Still, Blanqui's defense speech, while undoubtedly Jacobin, was not socialist. His solution to the inequities of the July Monarchy is the implementation of universal suffrage and the establishment of a representative government. This would allow for a fairer system of taxation. He said:

> Taxes must strike the unproductive consumers so as to stimulate the sources of production; taxes must facilitate the further reduction of the public debt, the purulent scourge of the country; finally taxes must substitute for the stock exchange's disastrous swindling with a system of national banks where active men will be able to find funds for investment. Then, but only then, will taxes be a benefit.[32]

Blanqui's taxation proposals would place great burdens on the rich, but this was not the same as calling for their expropriation. All in all, Blanqui's politics, for all their militancy, went little beyond other republican and Jacobin programs.[33]

The speech showed that Blanqui's understanding of the *proletariat* was not identical to the Marxist definition, meaning the industrial working class, but was more of a stand-in for the Jacobin concept of the *people*. Taken literally, Blanqui's claim that France was composed of thirty million proletarians would mean close to 90 percent of the population were workers. Blanqui's broad definition of the proletariat would have included not only the small industrial working class but also petit bourgeois elements such as the peasantry, shopkeepers, and artisans. These were the "people" invoked by the Jacobins. Blanqui likely adopted the term *proletariat* because it signified not just the old Jacobin meaning of the *people*, but it had another meaning: the most oppressed and virtuous class whose members desire "the overthrow of all castes and all tyrannies."[34] To stand with the proletariat was to join with the oppressed against tyrants and aristocrats in the cause of freedom. As a good Jacobin, that's where Blanqui's allegiance lay.

ASSESSMENT

Between the end of trial in February and the start of his imprisonment in March, Blanqui was allowed to remain at liberty. During that period, he delivered a speech to the Friends of the People. This speech crystallized his historical understanding of the July Revolution and the nature of class struggle between the workers and the bourgeoisie.

His speech, delivered on February 2, stated that "there is a war to the death between the classes that compose the nation."[35] Blanqui divided the classes of France into three parts: "that of the so-called upper classes, that of the middle or bourgeois class, and finally that of the people."[36] Then Blanqui analyzed the class struggles that took place following the Restoration when the bourgeois welcomed the installation of the Bourbons. According to Blanqui, the bourgeoisie were initially given equal rights alongside the aristocracy in the government. In 1825, the bourgeoisie turned against the Bourbons when Charles X

took a daring step towards the Ancien Régime and declared war on the middle class by proclaiming the exclusive dominance of the nobility and clergy under the banner of Jesuitism. The bourgeoisie is by essence anti-spiritual: it detests churches, and believes only in double entry bookkeeping. The priests irritated them: they had consented to share with the upper classes in oppressing the people, but seeing its turn arrive as well, full of resentment and jealousy against the high aristocracy, it rallied to that minority of the middle class that had combated the Bourbons since 1815 and that it had sacrificed up till then.[37]

From 1825 to 1830, the bourgeoisie fought the Crown to defend the rights of the Charter, but the people "remained a silent spectator to the quarrel, and everyone knows that its interests didn't count in the debates of its oppressors. To be sure, the bourgeois cared little about them and their cause."[38]

When the July Revolution came, Blanqui claimed:

> The people were the victors. And then another terror seized them [the bourgeois], more profound and oppressive. Farewell dreams of the Charter, of legality, of constitutional royalty, of the exclusive domination of the bourgeoisie! The powerless ghost that was Charles X faded away. In the midst of the debris, of flames and smoke, the people appeared standing on the corpse of royalty, standing like a giant, the tricolor flag in hand. They were struck with stupor.... You can see that during these days, when the people were so grand, the bourgeois were tied up between two fears, that of Charles X in the first place, and then that of the workers.[39]

Blanqui asked how the people were robbed of a republic in July. His answer was that:

> the combat was so brief that its natural leaders, those who would have led the way to victory, didn't have the time to distinguish themselves from the crowd. They necessarily rallied to the leaders who had figured at the head of the bourgeoisie in the parliamentary struggle against the Bourbons. What is more, they were grateful to the middle classes for their little five year war against their enemies, and you have seen what benevolence, I would almost say what feeling of deference they showed towards those men in suits they met on the streets after the battle.... Whatever the case, the masses hadn't formally expressed any positive political will. What acted on them, what had thrown them into the public square, was the hatred of the Bourbons, the firm resolution to overthrow them.[40]

Even though the people were denied victory, in surveying the current political scene, Blanqui observed:

> The people had suddenly entered the political scene that they took by assault, and though more or less chased from it at the same instant, they nevertheless acted with mastery. They withdrew their resignation. It will henceforth be between them and the middle class that bitter war will be carried out. It's no longer between the upper classes and the bourgeois: in order to better resist, the latter will need to call their former enemies to their assistance. In fact, for a long time the bourgeoisie has not hidden its hatred of the people.[41]

Since republicans and patriots were still persecuted, the July Monarchy showed that "two principles share France, that of legitimacy and that of popular sovereignty."[42] The first principle, that of royalist legitimacy, was condemned by Blanqui as "the ancient organization of the past. This is the framework society lived in for 1,400 years, and that some want to preserve by instinct of self-preservation, and others because they fear that the framework won't be able to be promptly replaced and anarchy will follow its dissolution."[43] The principle of popular sovereignty was identified in revolutionary terms as "rall[ying] all men of the future, the masses who, tired of being exploited, seek to smash the framework that suffocates them."[44] In the end, one or the other principle must triumph. Blanqui closed the door to any third alternative.

In looking at the international situation, Blanqui said that other nations "saw in the three days the awakening of the French people and the beginning of its vengeance against the oppressors of nations."[45] Blanqui believed the July Revolution should have unleashed a war of liberation against monarchs of Europe, reminiscent of the wars of the First Republic. However, the French bourgeoisie in league with foreign powers, who were fearful of a revolutionary war, betrayed the revolution. To Blanqui, a revolutionary war

> makes the bourgeois turn pale. Listen to them! War means bankruptcy, war means the Republic! War can only be supported with the blood of the people; the bourgeoisie doesn't involve itself in this. Their interests, their passions have to be appealed to in the name of liberty, of the fatherland's independence. The country must be put back into

their hands, which alone can save it.[46]

Blanqui's analysis showed a genuine attempt to identify the social classes in French society and the role each of them would play in a coming revolution. His view of the role of the bourgeoisie and aristocracy during the Restoration is largely accurate as far as it goes. The same can be said for Blanqui's verdict on the July Monarchy as a state serving the interests of the bourgeoisie, which has been recognized by many subsequent commentators such as Marx.

SOCIALISM

Until now, Blanqui's ideas were not particularly unique among those held by left-wing republicans and Jacobins. He shared with them a hatred of royalists and aristocrats. Alongside other radical republicans, Blanqui venerated Jacobin revolutionaries such as Robespierre and Saint-Just. His belief that universal enlightenment would be enough to instill a sense of virtue in the people and overcome the reactionary influence of the Catholic Church would not be disputed by Jacobins. Blanqui's speeches of 1832 did not propose expropriating the bourgeoisie; they proposed a new republic to institute fairer taxation on the rich to assist the workers. However, Blanqui was growing attuned to the conditions of the working class, and he had already encountered utopian socialism. By the time he emerged from prison in 1833, his socialist convictions had taken firmer shape.

The first expression of Blanqui's socialism can be found in *Le Libérateur*, a newspaper he founded in February 1834 that lasted only one issue. According to Blanqui, the goal of *Le Libérateur* was twofold:

> On one hand it will make an effort to expose in simple, clear, and precise terms why the people are unhappy and how they can cease to be so. It will explain the nature of the relationships that exist today between the master and the worker, the social question that virtually on its own constitutes all of political economy, and about which professors say barely a word. And at the same time, addressing itself to men whose profound meditations turn them from the hustle and bustle of the moment in order to embrace from on high all of

humanity in its past and its future, it will submit to them its critical views on the current organization, or rather, disorganization, as well as ideas on the principles that should preside over the re-composition of the social order.[47]

While the second issue of *Le Libérateur* never appeared, Blanqui did write an article, "Social Wealth Must Belong to Those Who Created It," where he laid out his new profession of socialist faith. In this article, Blanqui offered his own rudimentary theory of history and class struggle explaining the origins of inequality. According to Blanqui, there were only two sources of wealth in society: "It resides exclusively in intelligence and labour. Indeed, it is through labour and intelligence that society lives and breathes, grows and develops, and if these two forces were to withdraw from it for even a single moment it would immediately dissolve and all its members would perish as if through a sudden catastrophe."[48]

If it was true that intelligence and labor were the sources of all wealth, then how had inequality originally come about? Labor and intelligence could only create wealth through the mediation of a third source: land. While land should belong to everyone equally, this was not the case. Blanqui explained: "Through deceit and violence, some individuals seized this common land that we walk upon. Declaring themselves to be the exclusive owners of this land, they established through law that it will forever remain their property and that this right to property shall form the basis of the social order."[49]

After the land was expropriated from the people, the concept of private ownership spread to other instruments of labor linked to the land, such as capital. The spread of private property means

> that the immense majority of citizens . . . find themselves forced to toil on land whose produce they do not reap, and to enrich through their labour an idle minority that gathers up everything. And so neither the instruments nor the fruits of labour belong to the working masses but to a usurping aristocracy that consumes and does not produce.[50]

Blanqui described that the reality of the current society as one "founded on conquest and which divided the population into two categories, the victors and the vanquished, reserving the exclusive ownership of the land for the former while transforming the latter into vile cattle destined solely to work and manure the land of these monsters. The logical consequence of such an organization is slavery."[51] He noted that the forms of inequality, slavery, and property have changed throughout history. The advance of equality destroyed domestic slavery, but it was reborn in the fifteenth century with the growth of the African slave trade that he said was "a permanent affront to humanity."[52] After centuries of struggle against privilege by the champions of equality, the French Revolution abolished aristocratic principles and slavery. Blanqui observed that slavery could not be re-established in naked brutality. Instead, new forms of domination emerged:

> Servitude does not mean being the transferable slave of a man, or being a serf attached to his land; it means being completely dispossessed of the instruments of labour, and then being put at the mercy of those privileged groups who usurped them, and who retain through violence their exclusive ownership of these instruments that are indispensable to the workers.[53]

The monopolization over the instruments of labor by a small class of capitalists meant that the majority of workers are reduced to conditions resembling slavery.

> Even if they agree to leave their victims just enough bread to spare them from death they do so only out of self-interest, just as one might add a few drops of oil onto the cogs of a mechanism to prevent rust from causing it to break down. Moreover, it is in the interest of the wealthy that the workers are able to perpetuate their miserable flesh so as to bring into the world the children of the slaves who are destined one day to serve the children of the oppressors, and thereby continue from one generation to the next this dual, parallel inheritance of opulence and poverty, of pleasure and pain, that constitutes our social order.[54]

Since the workers are degraded and impoverished, they cannot understand the causes of their suffering but remain ignorant. Blanqui said this makes "them the docile instruments of the wicked passions of the privileged."[55] Since the rich control even the memory of the past, they teach the people "to spit on the tombs of these martyrs" for equality such as the Jacobins.[56]

Since history is full of struggle and revolts by the oppressed that threaten the system of inequality, the rulers have no recourse but to preach to the poor that they share common interests with the rich. Blanqui disputed the claim that there was a harmony of interests between the working class and the bourgeoisie. Rather, the latter enriches itself at the expense of the former. According to Blanqui, far from all classes of society sharing compatible interests, the opposite was actually true, and there were irreconcilable class differences with mutually conflicting interests:

> In the current state of things, it is certainly all too clear that the proletarians cannot survive twenty-four hours without the instruments of labour that the privileged control. But it is a strange form of reasoning to conclude from this that there is a community of interests between the two classes. We see nothing in this coupling but the union of the lion with the lamb. The classes only subsist on condition of boundless tyranny on the one hand and absolute submission on the other. But if the master strives constantly to make the chains that bind the oppressed heavier, the latter strive to free themselves from the yoke. What we have here is not a community, but rather a conflict of interests. There is no other relation between the two unequal halves of society than that of struggle, and their only need is to cause the other as much harm as possible—in a word, it is organized war.[57]

To fight the principle of property, Blanqui affirms the principle of equality that he said was first introduced in Europe by Jesus Christ. In the grand sweep of history, there were only two sides: that of equality and property. It was imperative to choose between them. As Blanqui said:

> In a word, we are always and everywhere with the oppressed against the oppressors, and we say with Saint-Just: "The wretched are the powerful of the earth." It makes no difference if oppression takes the form of military or commercial aristocracy, or if the people are exploited by the saber or the coin; our hearts are moved with the same pity for the sufferings of the peasant trampled by his master's steed as for the agony of the worker whose blood serves to oil the gears of his industrial overlord. Indeed, nothing has changed, except that privilege, defeated in the armor of a haughty baron, reappears in the garb of the capitalist. It is still privilege, with its same banner

of "Idleness and exploitation," and equality continues to oppose to it, with no less resolve, its motto that has so often proved victorious: "Intelligence and labour!"[58]

The long struggle of equality has advanced through the centuries due to popular struggle. It still remained necessary for the champions of equality to wipe out the remaining privileges in society to achieve full equality and "destroy all forms of exploitation of man by man."[59] Blanqui has faith that in the age-old struggle between property and equality that the latter will win:

> For if the right to property were destined to triumph, a bleak future indeed would appear before us. Humanity is not stationary; it either advances or it retreats. And the road forward goes towards equality. If it goes backwards it must necessarily retreat back up all the degrees of privilege right until personal slavery – the ultimate expression of personal right, and the ultimate expression of the right to property. . . . Fortunately, none of these things are to be foreseen, and we can, without any illusions, rest assured that all nations are advancing, with the French leading the way, towards the definitive conquest of absolute equality.[60]

Even though the word *socialism* had not yet entered his vocabulary, Blanqui used the utopian term *association* in its place. His vision of equality was not the Jacobin one of equal partition of land to create independent property owners but the common ownership of both the instruments of labor and land. Whatever name it was called, Blanqui's vision was now unmistakably socialist.

It was no longer enough for revolutionaries to call for a republic. Blanqui said that his republicanism was conditional in the hope that "the republic will succeed in implementing the social transformation that France so urgently calls for and which is its destiny. If the republic were to fail to fulfill this hope we would cease to be republicans, for in our eyes a form of government is not an end but a means, and we only want political reform as a step along the road to social reform."[61] A revolutionary's ultimate loyalty and faith lay not with the republic but with equality.

How to achieve equality? The experience of the July Revolution had proved to Blanqui that making surface modifications was not enough since they did not address the roots of inequality:

> As you see, citizen, we have in mind less a political change than a refoundation of society. The extension of political rights, electoral reform and universal suffrage may be excellent things, but only as means, not as ends. Our goal is the equal sharing of the burdens and the benefits of society; it is the complete establishment of the reign of equality. Without this radical reorganization all formal modifications in government would be nothing but lies, all revolutions nothing but comedies performed for the benefit of an ambitious few.[62]

Since the bourgeoisie still controlled the sources of economic power, reforms would never be enough to liberate the masses. He noted that whenever the workers assembled or "try to agree on means of relieving their common misery or of protecting themselves from their exploitation, they are thrown into prison for two, three, five years; they are hunted down; they are arbitrarily stripped of their employment records."[63] The capitalists also controlled the press to spread slander against revolutionaries since they are "powerless to fight against republicans through principles alone."[64] Nor would the existing state ever make genuine steps toward equality since it remained a "gendarmerie of the rich against the poor."[65] Blanqui believed that just as the aristocracy had not voluntarily relinquished their privileges in 1789, neither would the bourgeoisie. Considering the situation in France, the only path to socialism appeared to be through force.

When Blanqui was in jail, opposition to the July Monarchy erupted into open insurrection in the Parisian revolt of June 1832. After suppressing the revolt, the government declared a state of siege. Club members went into hiding, newspapers were closed, and the prisons filled.[66] Two years later, opposition coalesced around the Society for the Rights of Man, who had supplanted the Friends of the People. The Society evolved into a paramilitary organization with nearly four thousand members (75 percent working class) and plans to take armed action against the government. The Society of the Rights of Man proposed a Jacobin program of universal manhood suffrage, schemes to bring workers and producers closer together, fairer taxation, a more equal sharing of labor, the right to insurrection, and endorsement of the Declaration of the Rights of Man and of the Citizen.[67] To that end, they launched an abortive uprising in Paris in April 1834.

Blanqui kept his distance from the Society, considering it inadequate to the revolutionary tasks at hand. For one, Blanqui objected to its program, which supported regulating private property, not eliminating it. Secondly, the society's loose organizational structure and its toleration of different doctrines meant divided loyalties and a lack of discipline. If the state was going to be overthrown, something better was needed. Lastly, Blanqui believed a revolutionary organization needed more than unity around the goals of socialism and the republic; it needed plans for taking and exercising power. Blanqui found the answers to these questions in the experience of the Carbonari and Jacobin communist Philippe Buonarroti.

BUONARROTI

Philippe Buonarroti (1761–1837), was an Italian aristocrat and a Jacobin during the French Revolution. Following the Thermidorian reaction, Buonarroti was thrown into prison where he made the acquaintance of the revolutionary communist, Gracchus Babeuf (1760–1797). Buonarroti was quickly converted to Babeuf's ideas and became one of the central organizers of the Conspiracy of Equals in 1796.[68] The Equals planned to launch an insurrection in Paris to achieve the "common happiness, the aim of society"[69] and restore the Jacobin Constitution of 1793.[70] According to Buonarroti, the conspiracy viewed the Constitution as a "preparatory step towards a greater good" provided the right to property was removed.[71] Due to a police informer, the Equals' plans were uncovered and the members were arrested. After a lengthy trial, Babeuf was executed in 1797.

Buonarroti was held in prison until 1799, when Napoleon allowed him to go into exile. From 1799 to 1830, Buonarroti was involved in many underground revolutionary groups throughout Europe, such as the Carbonari.[72] In 1828, Buonarroti, now approaching old age, published *A History of Babeuf's Conspiracy for Equality*. This was not only an account of Babeuf's endeavor, but also the first great radical history of the French Revolution. Buonarroti's work is described by Ian Bichall as "a remarkable account of the conspiracy, setting out both its organizational practice and its socialist aims. His account . . . was simultaneously a personal memoir and a carefully documented history, the overall accuracy of which is unimpeachable."[73] In the first days after its release, Buonarroti's *History* sold more than 60,000 copies.

Before his death, Buonarroti was involved in the opposition to the July Monarchy, moving in the same circles as Blanqui. According to Alan Spitzer,

> They were both members of the revolutionary society of the Friends of the People in 1832; they both appeared on a defense committee for the Lyonnais and Parisians accused of fomenting insurrection in April of 1834. In 1835, Buonarroti wrote a letter in which he mentions Blanqui as a witness to certain of his actions.[74]

While there is no mention of Buonarroti in Blanqui's works, he did absorb important lessons to perfect his ideas on organization and revolution.

Buonarroti argued that a conspiracy, by its nature, could not be a mass organization, but must be composed of elite and virtuous revolutionaries. These men must be able to avoid the police and be skilled in the art of insurrection. The members of the conspiracy would be pre-selected based on their enlightened ideas and devotion to the people. Buonarroti said this revolutionary elite must be the instrument of liberation since the people were too ignorant and mystified by religion to free themselves. He said, "Never . . . has the mass of the people attained the degree of instruction and independence necessary for the exercise of those political rights that are essential to its preservation and happiness."[75] Once the conspiracy seized power, they would create a revolutionary dictatorship to defend the poor against the rich. The other task of the dictatorship was to educate the majority of ignorant and backward people in new values. Once these tasks were completed and the people were enlightened, the dictatorship would be finally replaced by the rule of the people.

While Blanqui may never have met Buonarroti, he assimilated his central ideas: the need for a conspiracy to conquer those in power, allowing the disciplined elite to then rule on behalf of the people.

THE SOCIETY OF FAMILIES

Increasingly, the space for legal opposition was being closed by the July Monarchy. Meetings of more than twenty were now prohibited by the penal code without prior police authorization. The sale of newspapers was restricted by a law passed in February 1834. More press laws were passed in September of 1834 that even carried the death penalty if newspapers simply published articles that could be regarded as advocating a change of government or the armament of the people, regardless of whether anyone took action. Following the April uprising, the July Monarchy stripped the population of the right to bear arms.[76]

By shutting down all legal opposition, the government had ended all disturbances, but Blanqui warned: "The silence of the streets is sinister, for it foreshadows a revolution. . . . Should a spark ignite the gunpowder, eighty thousand armed men will appear on the public square."[77] Now that Blanqui's ideas on socialism had crystallized, it was time for action.

During a trial for members of the Society of the Rights of Man, Blanqui met two key collaborators in his efforts to lay the groundwork for an effective conspiracy. One man was Martin Bernard, a Jacobin who detested industrialism and was influenced by Saint-Simonism.[78] The second was Armand Barbès, a wealthy law student and radical republican. According to Jill Harsin, Barbès was "loved because of his chivalric bravery, and would be revered because of his sufferings in prison."[79] Blanqui also recruited Eugène Lamieussens, who had directed a section of the Society of the Rights of Man. These three men, together with Blanqui, formed the nucleus for the insurrectionary communist conspiracy—the Society of Families.

The Society of Families was originally founded in July 1834 by Hadot-Desages, an obscure republican publisher. Shortly thereafter, Blanqui and his lieutenants took command and committed the organization to the seizure of power. Blanqui's vision was spelled out in the Families' oath: "Our tyrants have forbidden us the press and association. . . . When the hour has sounded, we will take up arms to overturn a government that has betrayed the country. . . . When the signal of combat is given, are you resolved to die, weapons in hand, for the cause of humanity?[80]

A series of questions and answers that initiated new members into the Families required them to identify the cause of oppression and the appropriate remedies:

> Q. What is the fate of the proletariat under the government of the wealthy?
> A. His fate is similar to that of the serf and the negro; his life is only a long tissue of misery, fatigue and suffering.
> Q. What is the goal that should serve as the basis for society?
> A. Equality . . .
> Q. Is it necessary to make a political revolution or a social revolution?
> A. It is necessary to make a social revolution.[81]

According to the Families, peaceful reform was not possible in France. The only solution for the workers and the country was the armed overthrow of the monarchy.

The Families were organized in the Babouvist and Carbonarist manner with a strict chain of command and small sections that only had limited knowledge of those above and below them. The cells also had no knowledge or contact with other cells. Very little was produced in the way of documentation in order to maintain the organization's clandestine nature. The Families were geared for revolutionary combat. According to Harsin, "Members were required to keep a supply of gunpowder and bullets; weapons were promised for the day of combat."[82] The organizational structure was designed to conceal the identity of its leaders, composed of Blanqui and his lieutenants.

At most, the Families numbered 1200. Its membership was a reflection of the Jacobin concept of the *people* with more than half being artisans, property owners, shopkeepers, and intellectuals.[83] The lack of working-class members did not bother Blanqui, since he believed that an elite of selfless revolutionaries can only be provided by bourgeois intellectuals:

> For there are, thank heavens, many bourgeois who have joined the proletarian camp. They are even what constitute its principal—or at least its most persistent—force. They bring to it an enlightened contingent that the people are unfortunately not yet able to provide

themselves. It was members of the bourgeois class who first raised the flag of the proletariat, who formulated egalitarian doctrines, and who now spread them, and sustain them, and restore them after they fall. Everywhere it is the bourgeois who lead the people in their battles against the bourgeoisie. [84]

Elsewhere, Blanqui wrote:

The bourgeoisie contains an elite minority, an indestructible phalanx—enthusiastic, zealous, ardent: this is the essence, the life, the soul and spirit of the Revolution. It is from this incandescent core that ideas of reform or renewal incessantly arise, like little bursts of flame that ignite the population. Who planted the proletarian flag? Who raises it up again after every defeat? Who are the promulgators, the apostles of egalitarian doctrines? Who leads the people into combat against the bourgeoisie? Members of the bourgeoisie.[85]

In Blanqui's conception, intellectuals served as leaders of the revolution and workers as shock troops.

The organization centered its operations in Paris for two reasons. The first one was strategic: Paris was the center of the government. Second, the history of previous French revolutions had shown that once power was taken in the capital, the insurgents could claim the authority to rule the country.[86]

In March 1836, the police located a secret gunpowder factory in Paris due to an informant. Thanks to another stroke of luck, during a raid of Barbès's apartment, they unexpectedly caught Blanqui. He managed to swallow incriminating papers before being arrested, but Barbès had papers in his possession that revealed the names and aliases of members.[87] Forty-three members were put on trial and hundreds were investigated. Blanqui was fined a large amount and put on trial. The Society of Families was broken.

During the trial, Blanqui ridiculed the ethos of the July Monarchy that placed him on trial: "Our only duty in this world is to enrich ourselves. The strongest and most cunning have free rein. Those who dream of universal happiness are either madmen or fanatics."[88] Blanqui proudly accepted that he was a "fanatic" for equality: "You have said that we are fanatics, and this appellation suits us well enough. . . . We have a faith, we have austere, passionate beliefs. We are not, thank

God, fleeting fair-weather republicans, enthusiasts one day, apostates the next."[89]

Once again, he denied the legitimacy of the count to judge him since the state existed to enforce exploitation: "None of the laws that are in force today rest on those eternal moral principles that have been deposited in the hearts of men, for the benefit and protection of societies."[90]

Blanqui reminded the court that Jesus had once been viewed as seditious: "Over the centuries, the cross, instrument of the cruelest and most ignoble torture, the object and symbol of opprobrium and infamy, nonetheless came to dominate the world, since on the cross there perished, some eighteen hundred years ago, another man whose judges also condemned as seditious."[91]

At one point during his defense, Blanqui said what truly frightened the July Monarchy was not the Society of Families, but the memory of 1789 and 1793: "It is the fearsome memory of our first revolution that is here evoked like a ghost in the eyes of the credulous and the timid, and that is punished in their minds by creating a threatening image of the future we hope to create."[92]

In August 1836, Blanqui was convicted along with other members of the Families for the illegal possession of arms. He was sentenced to two years in jail and two more under surveillance. Following a royal amnesty in May 1837, Blanqui was released and once more began organizing another conspiracy.

IV. Aux Armes!

The Society of Seasons

Blanqui's imprisonment at Fontrevaud was especially hard since he was separated from his family. Even though Blanqui was kept isolated in prison, he was allowed to assemble a small library on topics ranging from history to physiology to economics. Jérôme-Adolphe, now a professor of political economy, helped his brother acquire books. He hoped that intellectual pursuits and study would lead Auguste away from revolutionary politics and return to "a more composed state of mind."[1] He was to be sorely disappointed.

After his release, Blanqui moved to Pontoise on the outskirts of Paris, since he was now forbidden to live in the capital. Blanqui was excited to be reunited with his family again. However, he was not planning on leading an idyllic life of home and hearth. The struggle beckoned to him. Visitors came to his residence, and he began making long sojourns to Paris. Despite being watched by the police, Blanqui proved to be quite adept at discovering all manner of ways of eluding them.

Blanqui was growing concerned at the prospects of forming a new conspiracy because Barbès showed a declining interest in participating. Barbès was comfortable living in the south of France, enjoying his estate and the affections of his family. When Blanqui called upon him to return, Barbès reluctantly did so as a matter of honor.[2]

Blanqui persisted in his efforts, and by early 1839, he had organized a new conspiracy named the Society of Seasons. The Seasons were organized in the same hierarchical manner as their predecessor, the Families. At the lowest level was a six-man section known as a *Week*, led by a *Sunday*. Four Weeks formed a *Month*, led by a *July*, totaling twenty-nine men; three Months formed a *Season*, each led by a *Spring*, for a total of eighty-eight men; four Seasons made up a *Year*. In total, three Years were organized. At the top of the organizational pyramid was a triumvirate composed of Blanqui, Barbès, and Bernard.[3] Only the leadership possessed full knowledge of the membership.

If the Seasons were fully staffed, they would number 1,059 men, slightly less than the 1,200 who made up the Families. However, the historical evidence suggests that the Seasons did not have a full complement. According to Bernstein, "The strength of the Society was put at six or seven hundred in 1838, and at nine hundred in March 1839."[4] Allied to the Seasons was a small group of German exiles, known as the League of the Just, who would take part in the uprising of 1839.[5]

Meetings were held at irregular intervals. Sometimes the meetings involved Months, even entire Seasons in cafés, where their leaders delivered speeches. Every so often, the Seasons were called into the streets to be reviewed by their commanders. Every member took these calls seriously because they didn't know if such a review would include orders to begin the insurrection.[6]

Since the carrying of arms was outlawed, well-to-do members of the Seasons distributed money to a working-class cadre who purchased gunpowder in small amounts to make cartridges.[7] After the police arrested several conspirators in possession of gunpowder, this nearly scuttled the whole organization.

Considering the clandestine nature of the Seasons, it is difficult to determine their social composition. The evidence suggests that the Seasons contained a higher proportion of working-class members than their predecessor. Aside from Blanqui, all thirty-one members put on trial for their part in the 1839 insurrection were small shopkeepers or manual workers.[8] Historian Claude Latta analyzed data on 323 participants in the uprising who had either died or been arrested and found that more than 87 percent were identified as members of the working class.[9] While the defendants on trial may not be an accurate representation of the social composition of the Seasons, it does show that the insurrectionary tendency of the working class was now being reflected in underground revolutionary groups.

Like the Carbonari and the Families, the Seasons had their own elaborate initiation ceremonies and oaths for prospective members. The catechism of the Seasons was likely written by Blanqui; the wording was similar to his newspaper articles. The Seasons' oath can be said to represent the synthesis of Blanqui's Jacobin communism with all the elements present: republicanism, an elite membership, the armed seizure of power to create a revolutionary dictatorship, and the goal of an egalitarian society.[10]

According to the reception procedure, a new member was brought blindfolded into a room where he was addressed as "Citizen" and asked a number of questions about his name, age, profession, and so on. Then he was asked to consider carefully his commitment to the Seasons and warned that revealing any information would mark him as a traitor under penalty of death. Once agreeing to this, he was asked seven more questions and had to repeat back the expected answer to confirm that he agreed with the Seasons' goals:

> What do you think of royalty and kings?
> That they are as dangerous to humanity as the tiger is to other animals.
> What are aristocrats now?
> Aristocracy by birth was abolished in July 1830. It was replaced by the aristocracy of money, which is every bit as voracious as the preceding one.
> Should we be satisfied with overthrowing royalty?
> All aristocrats must be overthrown, all privileges must be abolished.
> What must we put in its place?
> The government of the people by the people, which is to say, the republic.
> Those who have rights without fulfilling obligations, as is the case with aristocrats, are they part of the people?
> They ought not to be part of the people; they are to the social [body] what a cancer is to the human body: the first condition for the return of the social body to a just state is the wiping out of aristocracy.

Can the people immediately govern themselves immediately after the revolution?

The social state being gangrened, heroic remedies are required to reach a healthy state; for a certain period of time the people will require a revolutionary power.

In summary, what are your principles?

Royalty and all aristocracies must be exterminated; to substitute in their place the republic, which is to say the government of equality; but, in order to achieve this government, to employ a revolutionary power, which enables the people to exercise their rights.[11]

If a member agreed with the principles, then he was asked to make the following vow to finalize his commitment:

In the name of the republic, I swear eternal hatred to all kings, all aristocrats, to all of humanity's oppressors. I swear absolute devotion to the people, fraternity to all men, aside from aristocrats; I swear to punish traitors; I promise to give my life, to go to the scaffold if this sacrifice is necessary to bring about the reign of popular sovereignty and equality.[12]

The Uprising of May 12, 1839

In early 1839, it appeared to Blanqui and his co-conspirators that the Orleanist regime was in a fatal crisis and that its day of reckoning was at hand. An economic crisis had caused production to stagnate and unemployment to rise to dangerous levels (150,000 were supposedly without work in Paris by the end of 1839).[13] After elections in March, Louis-Philippe was unable to form a stable cabinet, and the government seemed paralyzed.[14]

In retrospect, the crisis at the summit of power was not a symptom of the death throes of the dynasty. Rather, there was an eagerness among the rank and file of the Seasons for decisive action, no doubt heightened by a seeming political and economic crisis of the July Monarchy. Louis Blanc observed that the Seasons' impatience forced them to take preemptive action:

The conspirators were seized with a fatal restlessness and impatience; they longed to fight, and declared that they would separate if the word were not given to them to take up arms—the members of the committee felt themselves fatally entangled by circumstances. Their army was lost to them if it did not hurry them along with it, and an iron hand drove them down a declivity, up which there is no returning after a first rash first step.[15]

Blanqui felt that if the Seasons did not act soon, then there was a danger that ordinary members would begin to drift away.

The initial plan scheduled the uprising for May 5, but when sections gathered on that day for review, Blanqui dispersed them. He changed the date to a week later—May 12. For two reasons, Blanqui believed that the twelfth offered better chances for success. First, he had received news that the government was moving in new troops to replace the current garrison. These soldiers were unfamiliar with the layout and terrain, putting them at a disadvantage compared to the Seasons. Secondly, races were scheduled for May 12 at the Champ de Mars, and a portion of the police would be needed there for crowd control. Blanqui hoped to catch the monarchy by surprise and seize vital points in Paris before the enemy had time to organize.

Blanqui's organization for the uprising showcased his masterful grasp of insurrectionary and street-fighting tactics. He planned for the insurgents to quickly seize control of bridges, military garrisons, and armories. In regards to the construction of barricades, he provided detailed instructions on where they should be constructed, their height, and so on. As Bernstein observed: "Defense in depth was his purpose."[16] Blanqui's plan of battle called for taking the Hôtel de Ville (the seat of municipal government), the Paris Prefecture of Police, and the Prefecture of Seine. All of these positions were centrally located, and once the insurgents seized and fortified them, they could march out and rally the people. After the people were on their side, then the July Monarchy would fall, and power would pass to the revolution.

On Sunday May 12, close to 2:30 in the afternoon, the call to arms for the Seasons finally came. In a disorderly and undisciplined attack, the Seasons took control of a well-stocked armory near the rue Bourg-l'Abbé. Once the armory was taken, the men quickly fell in line behind their commanders. Barbès and his troops took the Palais de Justice, then moved on the Prefecture of the Police but encountered heavy resistance and fell back. They attempted to seize the Place du Châtelet, but enemy fire caused them to withdraw. Then, Barbès's contingent joined the main detachment moving toward the Hôtel de Ville. The insurgents successfully disarmed the soldiers protecting the Hôtel and occupied it.

Barbès went onto the balcony and read out a proclamation that Blanqui had written to explain the reasons for the insurrection:

> To arms, Citizens!
> The fatal hour has rung for the oppressors.
> The cowardly tyrant of the Tuileries laughs at the hunger that tears at the guts of the people. But the measure of his crimes is full. They are finally going to receive their punishment.
> Betrayed France, the blood of our murdered brothers cry out to you and demand vengeance. Let it be terrible, for it has delayed too long. Let exploitation perish, and may equality triumphantly assume its seat on the intermingled debris of royalty and aristocracy.[17]

The declaration named the military leaders of the insurrection whom the people were expected to obey: Blanqui (Commander-in-Chief), Bernard, Barbès, and other members of the Seasons. A provisional government was named that included the following names: Blanqui, Barbès, Bernard, Marc-René de Voyer de Paulmy d'Argenson, Hugues-Félicité Robert de Lamennais, Prosper-Richard Dubosc, and Albert Laponeraye. Of those listed, Dubosc and Laponeraye were members of the Seasons already in prison and had no knowledge of the insurrection. D'Argenson, a retired opposition politician, and Lamennais, a reformist Catholic priest, both denied they had anything to do with adding their names to the provisional revolutionary government.[18]

Even though the revolutionaries were optimistic about victory, they were hampered by a number of weaknesses. The number of insurgents was supposed to total more than a thousand, but they had a poor turnout. Estimates range from 150 to 600 revolutionaries who took part in the rising.[19] Key to Blanqui's plan was the element of surprise. He had hoped to catch the Parisian garrison—numbering 30,000—off guard and to overwhelm them in a popular upheaval. However, the garrison mobilized quickly, and by the early evening, close to a thousand troops were moving into the insurgent zone.

The carefully planned layout of barricades was unable to stem the government's advance. The monarchy retook the center of the city by nightfall. At the battle of Greneta, the revolutionaries fought bravely, where Barbès was severely wounded and captured. There was a last-ditch attempt the following day to resume the insurrection, but the garrison quickly overcame the revolutionaries. After two days of fighting, the Society of Seasons was crushed, and "order" reigned in Paris once again.

Blanqui had expected that a single heroic strike would awaken the revolutionary élan of the workers, and this would spread the revolt across Paris. Instead, the Parisian population watched in confusion on May 12, as the Seasons launched their insurrection, and they took no part in it. This was the fatal flaw in Blanqui's conception of revolution: the masses played no role in liberating themselves. As for the political crisis of the Orleanist Monarchy, it disappeared once the uprising began. A new government was soon formed, and the bourgeoisie rallied to the Crown. Blanqui remained in hiding until October 13, when he was captured trying to escape to Switzerland.

There were two trials for the revolutionaries. The first one, in June of 1839, contained nineteen defendants, among them Barbès and Bernard. All the accused were charged with instigating civil war to overthrow the Orleanist Monarchy. At trial, Barbès delivered a political defense and took full responsibility for his actions on May 12. At the end, Barbès was sentenced to death, but his dignified manner in court had given rise to public sympathy on his behalf. The Crown yielded to popular pressure and commuted Barbès's punishment to one of life imprisonment.

The second trial took place in January 1840. There were thirty-one defendants, including Blanqui. He attempted to invoke the right to revolution as his defense, but the court rejected this as illegitimate. For the rest of the trial, Blanqui offered no defense and insisted that he had "absolutely nothing" to say. He was found guilty and sentenced to death. Following the precedent set by Barbès, Blanqui's sentence was commuted to a life term at the fortress of Mont-Saint-Michel.[20]

V. L'ENFERMÉ

For nine years, Blanqui endured hellish captivity in the prison of Mont-Saint-Michel. The prisoners spent twenty-three hours a day in their cells that stank of excrement. The rules were strictly enforced by the warden, Theurier, who ran the prison as his own private fiefdom. Any questioning of the rules was answered with severe beatings. The prisoners found themselves locked in a semi-state of war with him. Blanqui refused to submit to the prison regime, writing to his mother: "When one is crushed by force, one must of course die when they kill you; but to submit willingly to humiliating measures when one can avoid them by making sacrifices, however great these might be, is a precedent that political prisoners must never establish."[1]

Those who broke the rules were taken to punishment cells located under the roof of the fortress. Almost every prisoner spent long stretches of time there. Blanqui once spent 127 days in one. It was impossible to properly sit or stand in these cells. During the winter, it was too cold, and in the summer, it was too hot. Prisoners went mad and attempted suicide in the face of such adversity. Previously strong, robust, and young men emerged from captivity old and emaciated with their health broken.[2]

On top of these conditions, Blanqui learned in February 1841 that his wife, Amélie-Suzanne, had died of a heart ailment at the age of twenty-six. For a year, Amélie-Suzanne had been ill, and when Blanqui was sentenced, she had unsuccessfully begged the prison authorities to see him. Her death devastated Blanqui, and he wept for weeks.

He appeared to contemplate suicide. One prisoner recorded Blanqui saying, "For my part, I no longer have much of anything to care about, nor much to fear; I no longer hold to life, it is a burden to me, that which remains will not last long, and I would wish only to exchange it for something."[3] For the rest of his life, Blanqui wore a black glove, covering a ring devoted to Amélie-Suzanne's memory, which he rarely removed. In articles written for *Candide* in the 1860s, Blanqui sometimes signed them with the pseudonym Suzamel in her honor.[4]

In another personal blow, Blanqui's surviving son, Estève, was taken in by Amélie-Suzanne's parents. Estève's grandparents raised him according to monarchist principles, antithetical to everything Blanqui believed. When Blanqui saw his son again years later in the late 1850s, there was an unbridgeable abyss between them. Estève offered to let his father stay with him, provided that he gave up politics. Blanqui refused. According to Bernstein, "the alienation scarred him permanently."[5] Blanqui still had his mother Sophie and two devoted sisters, Mesdames Barellier and Antoine, but this did not compensate for the losses he suffered.

It would have been easy for Blanqui to give in to his despair. Indeed, it would have been the most natural thing in the world for him to do. His wife dead, his son estranged, and his conspiracy crushed. He was locked away in prison by his greatest enemies. Blanqui remained unbowed and unbroken. He remembered the four dead Carbonari of 1822, the betrayed insurgents of July, and the suffering working class. He had made a commitment to the revolution and the ideal of a new world of equality. Whatever else happened, he would endure and hold high that banner. This was now his life's only cause, and he would see it through to the end.

Blanqui attempted to maintain his health and survive by subjecting himself to the same strict routine he learned in his younger years. He kept up his vegetarian diet and exercised constantly. Most of the time, Blanqui was alone with nothing to do except to read. He managed to renew contact with the outside world, through the intermediary of Fulgence Girard, a socialist-republican friend from school, who was now a respected journalist and lawyer. Blanqui described Girard's conduit to the world: "like a renaissance of the world; a resurrection from [his] tomb."[6] Girard not only brought him news but also smuggled out messages to his mother. Those messages contained detailed information on the conditions at the Mont-Saint-Michel that were publicized to the world. The campaign against the prison regime brought such great public pressure and outrage that Louis-Philippe issued a general amnesty for fifty-nine political prisoners in October 1844. In July of 1845, some of the harsher conditions of solitary confinement were removed and political prisoners were allowed to communicate for most of the day.[7]

Girard also became involved in one of Blanqui's plans to escape by sea to the British island of Jersey. Sophie assisted by bringing rope and tools in order to help Auguste escape. Blanqui, Barbès, and three others were to make the escape attempt. They planned out every detail from the methods of communication to the tunneling. On the night of February 10, 1842, the five men believed it was time to act. They removed the bars from one of the cells and lowered a rope. Barbès, the first to make the descent, ended up slipping and falling to the ground. The sound of his crash alerted the guards, and their attempt was thwarted. This failed endeavor led to renewed fighting between the prisoners and the staff. Prisoners were thrown into the punishment cells, and a new director arrived to discipline the populace. According to Bernard, the resolve of the prisoners was not broken; rather they were united by "holy solidarity, which was not only a duty for [them], but still more in conformity to [their] clearly understood interests."[8] The harsh prison regime and the brutality of the guards took its toll and ruined the health of many prisoners, among them Barbès and Blanqui.

In January 1844, Blanqui began exhibiting the symptoms of tubercular larynx. At the urging of doctors, he was moved from Mont-Saint-Michel to the more hospitable climate of Tours. Once Blanqui arrived there, the doctors examined him and concluded that his death was imminent. The Orleanist regime feared that the death of an intractable adversary such as Blanqui would create a martyr and enrage public opinion. Louis-Philippe decided to pardon him. When Blanqui received word of the royal pardon, he wrote a letter back to the authorities:

> Tell the gentleman that I proclaim solidarity with my comrades. Does he believe, by any chance, that the tortures of our imprisonment have

broken that solidarity? It was that which upheld us in our terrible struggle; it was that which has been our strength. Let the Minister send me back into the nearest prison. This prospect would be a pleasure to me, compared with that of an odious pardon.[9]

The news of Blanqui's refusal was widely publicized, contributing to his growing stature among the opposition.

The monarchy had another reason to treat Blanqui in such an indulgent manner; it provided the opportunity to discredit him and drive a wedge between him and other revolutionaries. Ever since the uprising of May 12, false stories about Blanqui had circulated claiming that he was "faithless and perfidious."[10] These stories of Blanqui's cowardice and malevolence were even repeated during his trial in 1840. While in prison, many captives formed cliques and grew hostile to him, some no doubt believing the rumors surrounding Blanqui. The ultimate effort to discredit Blanqui would be the release of the confidential Taschereau Document in 1848 that would split him from some of his closest comrades, such as Barbès (discussed in the following chapter). Blanqui declined the pardon in part because he had some inkling of the government's disinformation campaign.

Despite Blanqui's refusal, he was granted clemency anyway and miraculously survived his illness. By 1846, his health was restored, but he did not have a moment of respite. In 1846, bread riots broke out in Tours when the price was raised due to a wheat shortage. The government concocted a case based upon the evidence of a communist conspiracy centered on Blanqui, who had incited the riots. The case was so flimsy that Blanqui was acquitted twice.

From June 1847 to the February Revolution of 1848, Blanqui was always followed by agents of the police. He was forbidden to reside in Tours. The government let the populace know that they were not to converse with Blanqui or to rent him a room. According to Bernstein: "The object was to isolate Blanqui in a sea of silence or to goad him into guilt."[11] Despite being technically free, the monarchy continued to hound him.

On February 23, word reached Blanqui of street fighting in Paris which had toppled the Orleanist regime. Liberation had come, and spring was at hand. After years of imprisonment and anguish, his spirit soared at the news of revolution that promised the beginning of a new era. After hearing the news, Blanqui hastened from the provincial backwaters to Paris in order to take part in events.

Blanqui's long captivity, suffering, and courage had given birth to a legend. As Spitzer writes, "For nine years he lived the role for which he is probably best remembered—L'Enfermé, the imprisoned one, the suffering but uncompromising hostage."[12] Blanqui was seen by his devoted followers as the incarnation and unconquerable soldier of the revolutionary ideal, who received only contempt and jail from the powerful as his reward. His utter dedication and incorruptibility could not be denied by anyone. Blanqui's same fidelity to revolution caused him to be viewed as a sinister and evil Jacobin by everyone from reactionaries to moderate socialists. At the dawn of the Second Republic in 1848, Blanqui's arrival in Paris appeared to be a realization of these fears.

VI. 1848

THE SECOND REPUBLIC

The French Revolution of 1848 was the result of a severe economic crisis that caused business failures and widespread unemployment. The price of bread rose, and workers clamored for jobs. Even though the July Monarchy had endured a number of crises over the years, it had alienated large sections of the opposition, whether bourgeois republicans or revolutionary socialists. Republicans believed that the Crown had betrayed the revolution of 1830 by substituting one royal dynasty for another, as opposed to creating a republic. The working class and radicals saw the Orleanist Monarchy simply as a regime that served the interests of capitalists at their expense. There was also conservative opposition from the Bourbon Dynasty (the so-called Legitimists) and Bonapartists who saw Louis-Philippe as a usurper.

In 1847, cracks emerged in the July Monarchy, when it was revealed that high-ranking members of the government had speculated with public funds, practiced extortion, and looted the treasury. The domination and rottenness of the big bourgeoisie led to increased calls for reform and an expansion of the voting franchise. The reform campaign took the form of banquets that were first held in Paris in July 1847. This moderate movement quickly gained momentum as it spread across the country, with many workers attending. The Crown grew frightened at the sight of open opposition that energized the workers, so they banned a banquet scheduled in Paris on February 20. Two days later, workers, artisans, and students marched to the Chamber of Deputies, shouting for reform and singing the national anthem, "La Marseillaise." When the government sent soldiers to disperse these demonstrators, the troops fraternized with the crowd. Then the cavalry was sent in and they charged at the people. This assault did not break the resolve of the people, who returned the next day, waving red flags and demanding a republic. The moderate bourgeoisie were prepared to call an end to the movement, and the king seemed willing to compromise, but the people in the streets pressed on. A massacre of fifty demonstrators on February 23 caused the insurrection to become general throughout Paris. The next day, 1,500 barricades were built and arms were seized. Louis-Philippe, fearing that the soldiers stationed in Paris were no longer reliable, abdicated his throne, and a Second Republic was established.[1]

Already, there were two diametrically opposed visions for the Second Republic. The bourgeois republicans hoped to achieve their dream of a regime that guaranteed basic political and civil freedoms and that protected private property. The workers were distrustful of them and many wanted a Jacobin-style social republic that would overturn privilege and private property. Needless to say, the bourgeoisie was fearful of the working class and its potential threat to order and stability. The liberal deputy and historian Alexis de Tocqueville summed up these upper-class fears:

> I spent the whole afternoon in walking about Paris. Two things in particular struck me: the first was, I will not say the mainly, but the uniquely and exclusively popular character of the revolution that had just taken place; the omnipotence it had given to the people properly so-called—that is to say, the classes who work with their hands— over all others. . . . The people alone bore arms, guarded the public buildings, watched, gave orders, punished; it was an extraordinary and terrible thing to see in the sole hands of those who possessed nothing all this immense town, so full of riches, or rather this great nation.[2]

The Second Republic had, in the words of Marx, "finally brought the rule of the bourgeoisie clearly into view, since it struck off the Crown behind which capital kept itself concealed."[3] Workers had gained the republic and could now conduct their struggle for emancipation in the open. In the wake of the revolution, there was a flowering of radical and socialist clubs, newspapers, and posters across Paris.[4] A hundred schools of thought contended as the workers debated ideas from association to republicanism to socialism and the merits of the National Workshops.

The National Workshops were the brainchild of Louis Blanc (1811–1882). Blanc was a reform-minded socialist, who favored a system of cooperative production organized by the workers and heavily financed by the state that would peacefully overcome the contradictions of capitalism. In his 1839 work, *The Organization of Labor*, Blanc envisioned that cooperatives would "soon be so successful in every sphere of industry that not only workers but also capitalists would join them. After a certain time, without expropriation, without injustice or irreparable disruption, the principle of association would triumph over individualism and selfishness."[5] Blanc's plan gained popularity among workers still suffering from the severe economic crisis, since the cooperatives guaranteed their right to work.

The new provisional government included Blanc as a minister, where he proposed the creation of the Luxembourg Commission to organize National Workshops to provide immediate relief for the unemployed. Other ministers ratified Blanc's plan as a concession to the workers and to bolster popular support for the government. However, the provisional government viewed the National Workshops as just emergency measures, while the workers saw them as government guarantees of their rights to meaningful work and the promise of a just society.

Even though socialists Blanc and Alexandre Martin (a working-class representative known as Albert l'Ouvrier) were part of the provisional government, they were outnumbered by the remaining bourgeois members, who ranged from monarchists to moderate republicans. These ministers were determined to do everything possible to make the Second Republic acceptable to the bourgeoisie and the peasantry by reining in working class radicalism. Every effort was made to turn public opinion against the workers' desire for a social republic.[6] Capital went on the offensive to immediately roll back the gains of the workers and establish a business-friendly environment. The Bank of France worked to discredit the republic by stopping the flow of credit to manufacturers and merchants. The credit crunch sharpened the economic crisis. Members of the bourgeoisie blamed the mounting crisis on the concessions granted to the workers. The provisional government did not repudiate the debt of the Orleanist Monarchy but imposed a series of new taxes on the peasantry to balance the budget. According to Marx, this alienated the peasantry from the Second Republic:

> They had to pay the costs of the February Revolution; in them the counter-revolution gained its main material. The 45 centimes tax was a question of life and death for the French peasant; he made it a life-and-death question for the republic. From that moment the republic meant to the French peasant the 45 centimes tax, and he saw in the Paris proletariat the spendthrift who did himself well at his expense. Whereas the Revolution of 1789 began by shaking the feudal burdens off the peasants, the Revolution of 1848 announced itself to the rural population by the imposition of a new tax, in order not to endanger capital and to keep its state machine going.[7]

A clash between the workers and the bourgeoisie could already be seen in the dispute over the national flag. When the republic was proclaimed, there was a question over whether the flag would be red or the traditional tricolor. To the workers, the tricolor had become a symbol of bourgeois domination under the Orleanist dynasty. The red flag represented both socialism and the working class. A compromise was reached whereby the tricolor was adopted as the national flag, and a red rose was attached to the flagpole.

The terror of armed workers in Paris made the bourgeoisie anxious to build their own armed force. Even though the National Guard was one of the few forces available to the provisional government, it was not viewed as a match for the workers. To overcome that deficiency, the Mobile Guard was formed, numbering twenty-four battalions, composed of members of the lumpenproletariat and young workers, to maintain order in the capital. The republican Alphonse de Lamartine described the Mobile Guard as an "anti-socialist and anti-anarchist federation."[8] The existence of two opposed classes, just like the compromise between two different flags, could not last.

THE RETURN

When Blanqui arrived in Paris on February 25, he kept in mind the lessons learned during the Three Glorious Days of July 1830. Blanqui feared that the Second Republic risked following the same road by turning power over to the bourgeoisie, who would betray the interests of the people. As he wrote later:

> The Republic would be a lie if it were to be only the substitution of one form of government for another. It's not enough to change words: things must be changed.
>
> The Republic means the emancipation of workers, it's the end of the reign of exploitation, it's the coming of a new order that will free labour from the tyranny of capital.
>
> Liberté! Égalité! Fraternité! This motto that shone from the front of our buildings should not be a vain opera decoration.[9]

His position on the dispute between the tricolor and red flag left little room for doubt among the bourgeoisie that Blanqui was in favor of a social republic:

> The tricolor flag is no longer the flag of the Republic. It's that of Louis-Philippe and of the monarchy. . . . It has been twenty times bathed in the blood of the workers. . . . It is said it is a flag of blood. It is only red with the blood of the martyrs who made it the standard of the republic. . . . Reaction has already been unleashed. It can be recognized by its violence. The men of the royalist faction roam the streets, insults and threats in their mouths, tearing the red colors from the boutonnieres of citizens. Workers! It's your flag that is falling. Heed well! The Republic will not delay in following it.[10]

Blanqui's message supported the demands of the extreme left, but overall he remained remarkably restrained in his statements.

While Blanqui feared bourgeois treason, he did not believe that the moment was ripe to launch another uprising. Meeting with other thinkers upon his arrival, he discussed the chances of success for another popular insurrection. Blanqui urged patience, stating the government was bound to fall and that striking too soon would mean defeat:

> France is not republican; the revolution that has just taken place is a pleasant surprise and nothing more. If we were to seek to raise to power, today, names that have been compromised in the eyes of the bourgeoisie by previous political condemnations then the provinces will take fright.
>
> . . .
>
> Leave the men of the Hôtel de Ville to their impotence: their weakness is a sure sign of their fall. They have in their hands an ephemeral executive power; we, for our part, we have the people and the clubs, where we will organize it in a revolutionary manner, as the Jacobins once did. We must be ready to wait a few days more and the revolution will be ours! If we seize power by a bold assault, like thieves in the night, who can say how long our power might last? Beneath us, would there not be energetic and ambitious men, burning to replace us by similar means? What we need is the great mass of the people, the faubourgs rising up in revolt, a new 10 August.[11]

Blanqui believed that the creation of the Second Republic and its newly granted freedoms meant revolutionaries no longer had to operate underground. As Bernstein argues,

> The old conspirator was struck by the simple fact that the people had aims and the will to fulfill them. Their part in the February Revolution had proved their competence. They were undaunted and optimistic. . . . Such combatants were not the human mass that daring and romantic activists could pull into action. In fact they would be suspicious of an outbreak by a small minority.[12]

Instead, Blanqui decided to follow the Jacobin example by organizing a political club to mobilize the people to put pressure on the government. Should the government fail in keeping its promises, the club could be used to organize another uprising. At the end of February, he founded the Central Republican Club (CRC), which would soon be known as le Club Blanqui.

The Central Republican Club maintained a feverish activity and held meetings six days a week. The maximum attendance at their meetings was 500, with a minority coming from the working class. One of the most frequent and popular speakers at the CRC was Blanqui. Victor Hugo heard Blanqui speak once and described the scene:

With this, frequent ablutions, cleanliness mingled with cynicism, small hands and feet, never a shirt, gloves always.

There was in this man an aristocrat crushed and trampled upon by a demagogue.

Great ability, no hypocrisy; the same in private as in public. Harsh, stern, serious, never laughing, receiving respect with irony, admiration with sarcasm, love with disdain, and inspiring extraordinary devotion.

There was in Blanqui nothing of the people, everything of the populace.

With this, a man of letters, almost erudite. At certain moments he was no longer a man, but a sort of lugubrious apparition in which all degrees of hatred born of all degrees of misery seemed to be incarnated.[13]

Club debates were stormy, but, as Blanqui observed later, their overall membership was far from "given to raving violence."[14] On the whole, the Central Republican Club was committed to open discussion and mass action.

To create a broad-based united front of the left to fight reaction, the CRC championed mostly democratic demands. In the initial manifesto the club presented to the provisional government in March 1848, there were demands for freedom of the press, association, and speech. For Blanqui, the fight to expand political freedoms would enable revolutionaries to not only reinforce republican institutions but also give them more space to spread their ideas.[15]

The manifesto contained two demands with specific working-class emphasis. One condemned anti-union laws, and the second called for all unemployed workers to be organized into a national guard.[16] Even though Blanqui was willing to organize and agitate openly in the Central Republican Club, he ultimately believed that the bourgeoisie would only be overthrown by armed force. It was not petitions that had caused Louis-Philippe to flee, but masses of insurgent workers defending barricades with guns.

Blanqui had almost mystical faith in the ability of arms and military organization to usher in socialism. Three years later in "Warning to the People," Blanqui said:

Arms and organization, these are the decisive elements of progress, the serious method for putting an end to misery. Who has iron, has bread. We prostrate ourselves before the bayonets; they sweep up the disarmed crowd. France bristling with workers in arms means the advent of socialism. In the presence of armed workers obstacles, resistances, and impossibilities will all disappear.[17]

In the same warning, Blanqui said any government would be treasonous to the interests of the workers if it did not "disarm . . . the bourgeois guards, [and order] the armament and organization of a national militia of all workers."[18] While Blanqui was capable of adapting to mass politics, he still asserted that the final success of the revolution came through the barrel of a gun.

Blanqui refrained from organizing the CRC around the daily wants of the working class, such as wages and hours, since he feared that too great a focus on these issues would dull their political consciousness.[19] To him, Blanc's National Workshops had shown the danger of the workers being lulled into waiting for deliverance from the state, while they remained preoccupied with bread-and-butter issues. He asked, "Where in history has one seen peoples fighting to become wretched?"[20]

The other focus of the Central Republican Club was on the proposed date for elections to the National Assembly that would draw up a new constitution. The right wing wanted early elections, knowing that they could count on a sweeping conservative majority in the provinces. If the right wing won victory through universal suffrage, this would be a crushing political and moral blow for the left. On the other hand, the left-wing (whether neo-Jacobins, reform-socialists, or revolutionaries) wanted to delay the elections. Blanqui shared this position and believed that the Second Republic needed to propagate republican principles to the people:

> In the countryside all influence rests in the hands of the clergy and the autocracy. By systematically isolating individuals, a clever tyranny has stifled all spontaneity in the heart of the masses. The wretched peasantry, reduced to the condition of serfs, will become a stepping stone for the enemies who oppress and exploit them.
>
> We grow indignant at the thought that the oppressors can benefit from their crimes in this way. It is sacrilege to deceive ten million men about their own salvation, to wrest from their inexperience the sanction for their slavery. This would be all too insolent a challenge to the barricades of February.

The people do not know; they must come to know. This is the work of neither a day nor a month. Since counterrevolution alone has had the right to speak for fifty years, would it be too much to grant the people—who ask for only half of the podium, and who will not put their hands over their enemy's mouth—perhaps a year of freedom?

Light must shine into even the smallest hamlet; the workers must lift their brows bowed by servitude and rise from the state of prostration and stupor where the dominant castes hold them, their boot on their throat.

And do not say that our fears are illusory! The elections, if they are held, will be reactionary. This is the universal cry. The royalist party, the sole party that is organized, thanks to its long domination, will control them through intrigue, corruption and social influence. It will emerge victorious from the ballot box.

Such a victory would mean civil war![21]

In the midst of the crisis and the increasing radicalization of the workers, on March 13, the CRC voted unanimously to invite other democratic clubs to join a common front.[22] In the interests of unity, the new program dropped all demands except for two: postponing elections to both the National Guard and the constituent assembly. The next day, other clubs made similar motions and fifteen clubs created a central committee. Soon, over 300 labor organizations affiliated to the new federation of clubs. They drew up a list of demands that a delegation would present to provisional government. This list included the two Blanqui proposed and another one calling for troops to be withdrawn from Paris. When the government refused to receive their delegation, the clubs had no recourse except to call the people of Paris out for a demonstration on March 17.

A hundred thousand workers marched that day and caused government to formally concede to all the demands: elections were postponed for a few weeks and troops were withdrawn. The demonstration had caused the government to bow to popular pressure, but March 17 also served to widen the gap on the left wing between the moderates and revolutionaries. Louis Blanc, who had spoken on March 17, feared it would overstep the bounds of legality. He hoped to exclude extremists, such as Blanqui, who would prevent a peaceful outcome.[23] For Blanqui, the demonstration served to harden his distrust of the bourgeois leaders of the republic and the ineptness of the moderates.

While the growing split on the left gratified the conservatives and reactionaries, their position remained insecure. If a united left was not stopped, then the bourgeoisie feared there was a real possibility of a second revolution led by Blanqui and another 1793 that would sweep them away. Marx observed of the growing polarization in France that "the proletariat increasingly organizes itself around revolutionary Socialism, around Communism, for which the bourgeoisie itself has invented the name of Blanqui."[24] For the forces of order to prevail, Blanqui would have to be stopped.

THE TASCHEREAU DOCUMENT

Blanqui now became the target of a ferocious press offensive. Reactionaries painted him as Robespierre reincarnated. Incredible tales were spun surrounding Blanqui: that he was going to unleash a new reign of terror that would make 1793 look like child's play. The worst blow came on March 31, when the *Revue rétrospective* released the Taschereau Document that attacked Blanqui's very integrity by calling him an agent of the police. The document served three major purposes: it attacked Blanqui's credibility as a revolutionary, isolated him, and divided the far left.[25]

The document, released by an Orleanist official named Jules Taschereau, claimed that Blanqui had informed on his comrades in the Society of Seasons. The Taschereau Document built on the treacherous portrait of Blanqui painted by the prosecutor during his 1840 trial. As Bernstein observed, "Everything about the piece was designed to designate [Blanqui], its tone, its architecture, the testimony and the tendentious nature of the facts."[26] The document, filled with factual inaccuracies, was clearly based on the accounts of police agents and prosecutors. None of the document's claims were particularly new, but they had destructive effects on the revolutionary left. No subsequent historian or biographer has ever been able to prove that Blanqui was a police informer.[27]

The most immediate and devastating effect that came from the Taschereau Document was an open split between Blanqui and Barbès. Barbès had been bitter toward Blanqui since the foundation of the Society of Seasons, and the two had remained cold toward one another while imprisoned in Mont-Saint-Michel. Now the document's publication caused an immediate breach between them. Barbès believed the accusations contained in the document to be true and "thought the personal criticisms of the inner circles, the cutting sarcasm of the piece as a whole, sounded like Blanqui, a man distinguished by his 'irony.'"[28] The split between two leading revolutionaries affected the ranks of the left, preventing united action by the clubs and emboldening the right.

Blanqui wrote a detailed reply to Taschereau's slanders that appeared in print two weeks later. Blanqui's reply was co-signed by forty-eight former members of both the Society of Families and Seasons. Blanqui's reply began by denying that he wrote the document: "Blanqui, the supposed author, did not write it, didn't sign it. No sign reveals its origin or guarantees its authenticity."[29] He asked, what was the rationale for becoming an informer? His life was not threatened since he was not under threat of a death sentence. Nor did his supposed treason bring about a lighter prison sentence: "Mont Saint Michel and the penitentiary at Tours answer this question. Who among my companions has drunk as deeply as me from the cup of anguish?"[30] Blanqui did not receive any handsome fortune for his supposed treason—he had little money to his name and currently was living in an attic.

Blanqui believed that these slanders were being leveled at him due to his effectiveness at mobilizing the people to recognize and confront reaction. He wrote, "What is my crime? That of having confronted counter-revolution, of having unmasked its plans for six weeks, and of showing the people the danger around them that is growing, and that will engulf them all."[31] As far as Blanqui was concerned, the royalists were the originators of the lies against him and they were not to be trusted. For them, "all methods were good in crushing a dangerous rival."[32] Blanqui warned that republicans who might believe the Taschereau Document:

> Republicans, old soldiers of the old cause who have remained faithful
> to the flag of principle, you who haven't sold your consciences to the
> new masters in exchange for honors, money or positions, beware! Let
> my example be a warning to you. Today it is me, tomorrow it will be
> you. Woe on those who cause embarrassment. We will all be struck!
> In the head, the heart, in front, from behind it doesn't matter: we will
> be struck![33]

More than 100,000 copies of Blanqui's reply were printed and distributed throughout the capital in early April. Blanqui's reply placed
both his accusers and the government on the defensive. Others on the
left such as Pierre-Joseph Proudhon, Étienne Cabet, and François-
Vincent Raspail were largely satisfied with Blanqui's reply.[34] Taschereau
took Blanqui to court for calling the document a forgery. The trial went
against Blanqui, but it had the ultimate effect of vindicating him. Most
of the witnesses were royalists who offered conflicting testimony. The
Taschereau Document was shown to be a copy of a copy. The original
could not be produced even though the court declared "its existence
in 1839 could not reasonably be questioned."[35] The final ruling against
Blanqui occurred because royalist witnesses were trusted more than
him. The trial left a number of questions unanswered: if the document
was so damning, why wasn't it used at other trials? The only possible
answer was that it was a forgery written in 1848 to discredit Blanqui.

MAY 15

While Blanqui was dealing with the slanders of the Taschereau Document, he continued to work on unifying the left. Continued political
and economic turmoil led to another radical mass demonstration on
April 16. By this time, the workers saw the National Workshops as
a farce, paying them a daily wage of two francs that was not enough
to provide for their families. The Luxembourg Commission planned
for the march to the Hôtel de Ville with a petition demanding that
the workshops be replaced with the true organization of labor that
would end the exploitation of man by man. In other words: socialism.
The organizers planned a peaceful demonstration, but the government

believed that the radicals intended to take power. Blanqui was in attendance at the demonstration, but according to his own account, he was there just to distribute his response to the Taschereau Document. The provisional government took preemptive action and spread a rumor that moderates had been killed. In response, the Ministry of the Interior called out 100,000 National and Mobile Guards who surrounded the protesters and shouted at them: "Down with the Communists! Down with Louis Blanc, with Blanqui, with Raspail, with Cabet!"[36] The events of April 16 had given the government an excuse to move reliable troops to the capital to deal with any future disturbances. The right was jubilant, celebrating openly in the Chamber of Deputies.

The worst fears of Blanqui and the left wing on the danger of holding early elections were realized following the results on April 23. Out of 880 seats to the Constituent Assembly, the Party of Order (composed of monarchists and conservatives) won 200 seats, the moderate republicans won 600 seats, and the democratic socialists won 80 seats. Even though the moderate republicans possessed a majority, nearly 300 of them had not been republicans before the February Revolution.[37] Of the 34 left-wing candidates nominated in Paris, only 6 of them were elected, mostly due to their name recognition. Barbès was elected in one of the Parisian departments. Blanqui himself won only 20,000 votes and was not sent to the Assembly.

In the run-up to the election, fighting had broken out between workers and the National Guard in both Limoges and Rouen. Blanqui decried the shooting of workers in Rouen:

> For the past two months the royalist bourgeoisie of Rouen has plotted in the shadows a St Bartholomew's massacre of the workers. It had stocked up on cartridges. The authorities knew of this. Calls for death had broken out here and there, the warning signs of the catastrophe. *We must have done with these scoundrels!*
>
> ...
>
> You know full well that there was no battle: it was a slaughter! And you let the slaughterers recount their feats of prowess! Is it that in your eyes, as in those of kings, the blood of the people is nothing but water, good for washing down the overcrowded streets from time to time? If so, then erase from your buildings that detestable three word lie that you have just inscribed on them: Liberty, Equality, Fraternity![38]

The workers and radical clubs in Paris continued agitating in the streets and writing manifestos. In light of the election results and the repression, the Central Republican Club debated a motion to reconsider organizing a new secret society.

Blanqui had not made up his mind about organizing a new secret society or preparing for a new armed confrontation when larger events forced his hand. On May 15, radicals planned to deliver a petition to the National Assembly for France to declare war on both Russia and Prussia if they did not immediately grant independence to Poland. The initial planning for the demonstration began on May 8, and Blanqui only learned of it a few days later on May 13. According to Jill Harsin, he argued against "his club's participation, on the grounds that the manifestations of March and April had caused public opinion to 'retrograde.' He had acceded only when he realized that his membership was overwhelmingly in favor."[39]

On May 15, approximately fifteen thousand demonstrators, led by a hesitant Blanqui, marched to the National Assembly. The leaders of the demonstration were openly flaunting the law since the direct presentation of petitions to the government was now forbidden. In the midst of the confusion, the radicals invaded the Assembly and proclaimed the establishment of a new revolutionary government. The military forces at the disposal of the government were completely confused by the turn of events, and units received no orders to arrest the radicals. Inside the National Assembly, there was utter chaos with several leaders attempting to bring order. Blanqui spoke at one point, arguing for the independence of Poland, and then tried to leave, but many urged him to speak about domestic repression and the needs of the workers. Blanqui's appearance at the Assembly was described by Alexis de Tocqueville:

> It was then that I saw appear, in his turn at the rostrum, a man whom I never saw save on that day, but whose memory has always filled me with disgust and horror. His cheeks were pale and faded, his lips white; he looked ill, evil, foul, with a dirty pallor and the appearance of a mouldering corpse; no linen as far as one could see, an old black frock-coat thrown about spindly and emaciated limbs; he might have lived in a sewer and just emerged from it. I was told that this was Blanqui.[40]

Not wanting to be outdone by Blanqui, Barbès spoke next and argued for creating a revolutionary government. Then a new provisional revolutionary government was proclaimed, containing the names of Blanqui, Barbès, Blanc, Pierre Leroux, and several other radicals. The new government was short-lived. After three hours of confusion, the National Guard finally found their footing and retook the building.[41] Key leaders of the demonstration were arrested on the spot, while Blanqui evaded arrest for eleven days. After Blanqui was picked up, he was sent to the prison of Vincennes to await trial.

The May 15 uprising was only a prelude to an even bloodier showdown in June. The catalyst came on June 22, when the provisional government abolished the National Workshops. The workers saw no choice but to take up arms once more. For the next four days, Paris was torn by civil war as the workers threw up barricades in three areas: the Latin Quarter, in the north and east, and on the eastern right bank. The two sides were unevenly matched. The minister of war, Louis-Eugène Cavaignac, proclaimed a state of siege in the capital and assembled an armed force of more than 150,000 National and Mobile Guards from Paris and its environs to crush the revolution. Cavaignac faced at most 50,000 workers, who possessed neither plans, nor supplies, nor allies. After four days of fierce fighting, the workers were utterly crushed. The death toll numbered in the thousands, and more than 14,000 were thrown into prison and 4,000 were deported to distant prison camps and the colonies.[42]

It is possible that the June insurgents could have defeated Cavaignac and the National Guard, but they had no leadership or organization. Blanqui was already in jail. The coup of May 15 came too soon, and as Marx noted, it "had no other result but that of removing Blanqui and his comrades—that is, the real leaders of the proletarian party—from the public stage."[43]

VII. The Mountain is Dead

Warning to the People

O n March 7, 1849, Blanqui, Barbès, Raspail, Blanc, and a dozen other socialist and revolutionaries stood trial before the High Court of Bourges for their involvement in the May 15 coup. The prosecution argued that Blanqui was the main instigator of popular disturbances against the Second Republic. At one point, a correspondent of *le Peuple* dubbed him the Evil One.[1] In his defense, Blanqui explained that he had attended the demonstration of May 15 against his better judgment and denied that he intended to overthrow the government:

> An armed attack on the Assembly, a violation of all our principles, would have remained as an indelible stain upon our past, and would have eternally weighed us down like a ball and chain. . . . The populace would not have been our accomplice in one hour of madness. Having dissolved the Assembly, we would have to face the masses who were not all prejudiced against it. . . . Neither Paris nor France would have relished the affair, and at the end of three days, perhaps, this counterfeit, unasked-for government would have ignominiously been overthrown.[2]

Blanqui said he tried to calm the protesters but reminded the court that an angry crowd was not so easy to control: "The point is that handling a popular element is not like commanding a regiment that stands ready arms in hand, to which you say 'march' and it marches, 'stop' and it stops. No gentlemen, it isn't like this at all."[3] On the last day of trial, the Taschereau Document was brought up and Barbès publicly attacked Blanqui in court.

When the verdict was delivered on April 2, six of the thirteen defendants were acquitted. Barbès and Blanqui were both found guilty. The former received a life sentence, and the latter a term of ten years. Less than two weeks after his conviction, Blanqui arrived at the fortress of Doullens, located in Picardy. Like most of the places where Blanqui was imprisoned, the conditions at Doullens were poor, with undrinkable water and cells without proper ventilation. Doullens was not as horrid as Mont-Saint-Michel, since the prisoners could garden and have food brought in from the outside.

By order of the Ministry of the Interior, Blanqui remained under close surveillance. The authorities believed he was contributing articles to a socialist journal, *les Veillées du peuple,* and they wanted to discover incriminating evidence on him. At one point, the guards entered Blanqui's cell and searched his papers. When a guard picked up a valued family letter, Blanqui became enraged and snatched it away. In the ensuing struggle, he was badly beaten. Later, Blanqui wrote a long letter to the attorney general demanding legal protection from the prison confiscating his personal possessions. His request was ignored.

While in prison, Blanqui maintained the same strict daily routine and a heavy reading load (the topics ranged from parliamentary debates to astronomy). It was important to Blanqui to stay in contact with his comrades on the outside, which was naturally done clandestinely. According to Bernstein, the process "required painstaking application. Before letters and articles were smuggled out of the citadel, they had to be written covertly, in invisible ink. Thin paper, yet strong in texture, was indispensable."[4] Blanqui's ever-faithful mother and sisters could be relied upon to smuggle out his messages.

On October 20, 1850, after only a year in Doullens, Blanqui and Barbès were transferred to the prison of Belle-Île. This penitentiary was located on a small island in northwest France, where the authorities could keep a more watchful eye on the prisoners. At Belle-Île, Blanqui had as much trouble with his fellow inmates as he did with prison officials. His feud continued with Barbès, causing the prisoners

to split into two irreconcilable factions. Joint classes on political economy and history were marred by mutual denunciations between the two
groups. At one point, the struggle caused open fighting to break out.[5]

In 1851, dissension between Blanqui and Barbès affected politics
outside of Belle-Île's walls at a banquet to commemorate the third
anniversary of the February Revolution. The banquet was organized
by French exiles in London, such as Louis Blanc, and included the
German revolutionaries August Willich and Karl Schnapper among
its participants. The program of the event was loose but had nothing
objectionable to Blanqui's principles. Still, the banquet angered Blanqui due to the participation of Louis Blanc (a friend of Barbès). Blanqui, invited to write a friendly toast, instead responded with an angry
denunciation of Blanc, entitled "Warning to the People." The event
organizers suppressed Blanqui's address, but the press broke the story, causing a scandal. The warning was given extra publicity by Marx
and Engels, political opponents of Blanc, Willich, and Schnapper, who
were angered at the suppression of Blanqui's address. They published a
German translation of Blanqui's speech in an edition of 30,000 copies.[6]

The main argument of Blanqui's "Warning to the People" was
that Blanc and other Jacobins, republicans, and democratic socialists
in the provisional government were traitors to the 1848 revolution
and remained a menace to future revolutions: "What obstacle threat-
ens the revolution of tomorrow? It is the same obstacle that blocked
the revolution of yesterday—the deplorable popularity of bourgeois
disguised as tribunes. . . . Sinister names written in blood on all the
paving stones of democratic Europe."[7] Blanqui blamed these moderates and the provisional government for delivering the Second
Republic over to the reactionaries:

> It is upon its head that the responsibility for all the disasters, for the
> blood of so many thousands of victims, must fall. Reaction simply
> followed its vocation when it slit democracy's throat. The crime was
> committed by the traitors whom the trusting people had accepted as
> guides and who then delivered them into the hands of reaction.
>
> . . .
>
> It and it alone must bear the terrible burden of all of the calamities
> that have all but wiped out the revolution!

Oh! they are the real culprits, the most guilty of the guilty—those whom the people, deceived by the words of tribunes, saw as their sword and shield; those they enthusiastically proclaimed to be the arbiters of their future.[8]

The Warning further inflamed hatred with Barbès and his allies at Belle-Île. Friends of Blanc were shocked by Blanqui's vitriol. Even Blanqui's comrades such as Pierre Leroux did not agree with the Warning.

Blanqui's "Warning to the People" and the experience of 1848 were signs that his political thinking was not only more overtly socialist but his opinions on Jacobinism were changing. For Blanqui, the political descendants of the Jacobins had proven themselves counterrevolutionary in 1848. The proof of this could be found in Alexandre Auguste Ledru-Rollin, one of the leaders of the neo-Jacobins. Blanqui especially hated Ledru-Rollin as minister of the interior, who used his position to organize the anti-socialist Club of the Revolution as a counterweight to Blanqui's federation of clubs.[9] On May 15, Ledru-Rollin had sided with the Party of Order against the abortive revolutionary coup. This was all enough for Blanqui to condemn Ledru-Rollin and other neo-Jacobins as traitors to the revolution.

In 1849, Blanqui wrote "To the Mountain of 1793! To the Pure Socialists, Its True Heirs!" where he denounced Ledru-Rollin and the neo-Jacobins for betraying the legacy of Robespierre: "Are these Montagnards nothing but Girondins? But I read the name of Robespierre on their hats."[10] The original Jacobins had been defenders of the people, who "loved those who suffer and hated those who caused suffering."[11] According to Blanqui, Ledru-Rollin and the latter-day Jacobins could not uphold this heritage, explaining, "The world has moved on in fifty years, but they have remained immobile. Science has forged more certain weapons, cleared a wider and more direct road. But the Mountain persists in walking down the paths of the past in old worn out attire, and they cry out against any novelty unknown to our fathers."[12]

The "more certain weapons" of the present that Blanqui specifically had in mind was socialism. Now that neo-Jacobinism had been discredited, it fell to the socialists to carry the revolutionary banner of 1793. Blanqui ended his article by declaring, "Citizens, the Mountain is dead! To socialism, its sole heir!"[13]

Based on his readings of the French Revolution, Blanqui believed it provided the model of class struggle that was repeated throughout history. On one side were the oppressed or the "plebs," whose destiny was "to work, suffer and die." Blanqui observed that every so often, such as in 1789, the "oppressed rise up in the face of such effrontery and ingratitude; they begin to struggle against this impudent aristocracy of parvenus."[14] After the French Revolution, the class struggle continued to occur, but it remained locked into the same sequence:

> Whoever now reads the history of our first Revolution also reads about our own current affairs. The events may differ, but the fundamentals remain identical. Interests, passions, language, episodes, everything looks the same. The people of that time have come back to life today. Our own self-styled Montagnards are a caricature, indeed a very poor copy, of the Girondins.[15]

Based on this interpretation of history, Blanqui was able to conclude that the conflict of 1793 had "just begun to start up again in this year of 1848, on the same battlefield, between the same combatants and, strange as it might seem, with almost the same daily episodes."[16] The difference was that now the revolutionary mantle had been taken up by socialism.

While Blanqui had upheld Robespierre in opposition to Ledru-Rollin, the experience of 1848 was causing him to become more critical of the former as well. Blanqui's skepticism of Jacobinism was reinforced after reading Alphonse de Lamartine's anti-Jacobin *Histoire des Girondins* (1847) in prison. Now he condemned Robespierre as "the successor of Torquemada," "a premature Napoleon," and "a herald of counterrevolution." The most unforgivable act for the staunch atheist Blanqui was Robespierre's creation of the Cult of the Supreme Being, which he believed restored religion. Blanqui concluded, "Robespierre killed the Revolution in three blows: the scaffold of Hebert, that of Danton, the altar of the Supreme Being. Struck to death, she stumbled, staggered for a few moments and fell and would not rise again. The victory of Robespierre, far from rescuing [the revolution], would have been for her only a deeper and more irreparable collapse."[17] Now Blanqui shifted his revolutionary allegiance from Jacobinism to the Hébertists, whom he hailed as the "most noble and vilified" forces of the French Revolution (discussed in Chapter VIII).[18]

In an 1852 letter to a republican exile, Georges Maillard, Blanqui's identification of revolution and socialism in place of Jacobinism became more explicit. Blanqui said that the word *democrat* has no meaning: "Is there any shade of opinion that could not somehow manage to find its place beneath this banner? Everyone claims to be a democrat, aristocrats above all others."[19] Blanqui claimed that words such as *republican* and *revolutionary* had become so debased by this point that they had been adopted by reactionaries. Blanqui believed it was time for the true republicans and revolutionaries—the socialists—to realize that the

> so-called Montagnards, with Ledru-Rollin at their head, are Girondins, and faithful copies of their predecessors. They have adopted, it is true, the motto and the banner of the former Mountain; they swear only by Robespierre and the Jacobins. But in this they have no choice. How would deception be possible without it? It is the common ruse of the schemers to wave the flag of the people.[20]

He clearly stated that in the current day, "You are a revolutionary-socialist; one cannot be a revolutionary without being a socialist, and vice versa."[21] If revolutionary socialists were going to carry on the French Revolution, then they must take the side of the workers in the class struggle. For Blanqui, it was imperative that socialists fulfill their historical role by leading the oppressed against tyrants like Napoleon III, who had overthrown the Second Republic in 1851.

Napoleon III

Even though the workers were defeated in the June revolt, this did not bring stability to the Second Republic. The moderate republicans were discredited among the workers for their support of Cavaignac. The center could no longer hold, and the National Assembly found itself divided between a royalist right and a socialist left. The Second Republic proved itself unable to deliver the bourgeoisie from popular upheaval. Internal conflicts among the bourgeoisie now threat-ened the very stability of society. In order to preserve its own rule as a class, the bourgeoisie had to, according to socialist author Hal Draper, "yield up direct political power to other and firmer hands, the better to safeguard its socioeconomic rule."[22]

Considering the unstable nature of the Second Republic, the bourgeoisie found itself obliged to strengthen the executive to main-tain order. As Marx says of the bourgeoisie, "In their uninterrupted crusade against the producing masses they were, however, bound not only to invest the executive with continually increased powers of repression, but at the same time to divest their own parliamenta-ry stronghold—the National Assembly—one by one, of all its own means of defense against the Executive."[23]

Louis-Napoléon Bonaparte (1808–1873), nephew to Emperor Napoleon, stepped into this political vacuum to save the bourgeoisie. Paradoxically, Louis-Napoléon also appeared to the people as their champion. In 1851, Friedrich Szarvady described Louis-Napoléon as follows: "He is a socialist with Proudhon, a reformer with Girardin, a reactionary with Thiers, a moderate republican with the supporters of the republic, and an enemy of democracy and revolution with the legitimists. He promises everything and subscribes to everything."[24] Bonaparte found a base of support from the small-holding peasantry whom the Second Republic had alienated. Marx explains how the conditions of the peasantry led them to support Bonaparte:

> Insofar as millions of families live under economic conditions of existence that separate their mode of life, their interests and their culture from those of the other classes, and put them in hostile opposition to the latter, they form a class. Insofar as there is merely a local interconnection among these smallholding peasants, and the identity of their interests begets no community, no national bond and no political organization among them, they do not form a class.
>
> They are consequently incapable of enforcing their class interests in their own name, whether through a parliament or through a convention. They cannot represent themselves, they must be represented. Their representative must at the same time appear as their master, as an authority over them, as an unlimited governmental power that protects them against the other classes and sends them rain

and sunshine from above. The political influence of the small-holding peasants, therefore, finds its final expression in the executive power subordinating society to itself. Historical tradition gave rise to the French peasants' belief in the miracle that a man named Napoleon would bring all glory back to them.[25]

Bonaparte's support from a myriad of classes allowed him to be elected president of the French Republic with 5.4 million votes (or nearly 75 percent of the total) on December 10, 1848. Despite this victory, Louis-Napoléon did not have total power, since the president of the Republic's term was limited to four years.

While Bonaparte owed his position to the support from the masses, he had a decided authoritarian streak. This could be seen in the Society of December 10. Organized in 1849, the society was a precursor to fascist gangs of the twentieth century in many respects. It was made up of members of the lumpenproletariat, declassed elements whom Marx called "refuse of all classes."[26] The Society served as Bonaparte's shock troops who silenced all opposition to his rule.

Napoleon's rise to absolute power was aided by a favorable set of circumstances. Bonaparte was able to outmaneuver opposition in the National Assembly and secure control of the army. The National Assembly's loss of control over the army had shown the bourgeois Party of Order "that the bourgeoisie has forfeited its vocation to rule. A parliamentary ministry no longer existed. Having now indeed lost its grip on the army and National Guard, what effective means remained to it with which simultaneously to maintain the usurped power of parliament over the people and its constitutional power against the president? None."[27] The republican opposition attempted to curb Napoleon's power by abolishing universal suffrage, re-instituting press censorship and refusing to extend the presidency's term. When the Assembly rejected appeals to restore universal suffrage, Bonaparte demagogically presented himself as a champion of universal suffrage and condemned the Assembly, winning him support from the people.

On December 2, 1851, after months of stalemate, things came to a head. After the Assembly rejected another proposal to restore universal suffrage, Bonaparte declared a state of siege and dissolved parliament. He also rescinded the voting restrictions and held a plebiscite that ratified his coup d'état by a wide majority. After becoming dictator of France, Bonaparte reassured the bourgeois forces of order that "the era of revolutions [is] closed."[28] The army quickly put down sporadic resistance to the coup in Paris and the provinces.[29] Exactly a year later, Louis-Napoléon solidified his position with another referendum that officially ended the Second Republic and began the Second Empire with himself as Emperor Napoleon III.

The Second Empire came into being as a state seemingly standing above all classes. As Marx noted, this was deceptive:

> The empire, with the coup d'état for its birth certificate, universal suffrage for its sanction, and the sword for its scepter, professed to rest upon the peasantry, the large mass of producers not directly involved in the struggle of capital and labor. It professed to save the working class by breaking down parliamentarism, and, with it, the undisguised subserviency of government to the propertied classes. It professed to save the propertied classes by upholding their economic supremacy over the working class; and, finally, it professed to unite all classes by reviving for all the chimera of national glory. In reality, it was the only form of government possible at a time when the bourgeoisie had already lost, and the working class had not yet acquired, the faculty of ruling the nation.[30]

During the Second Empire, capitalism was given free rein to develop and expand in a way not seen under previous regimes. From 1852 to 1857, the state financed a rapid expansion of railroads, engineering, and metallurgy. Mergers were encouraged in all these sectors of industry. In just five years, industrial production increased by 50 percent. The trend of industrial development was unmistakable.[31]

It was the emperor's hope that economic growth would blunt class conflict. Nominal wages did rise 20 percent by 1870, but a rise in the cost of living offset these gains. [32] Despite the denial of political freedoms, there were still working-class organizations. The police kept a close watch on them, as evidenced by 4,000 arrests for violating anti-union laws from 1853 to 1866.[33] Repression did not work, and after 1864, the emperor granted a series of reforms to co-opt workers, such as legalizing unions and strikes along with relaxing censorship. While workers now had greater freedom to organize, the army was put at the disposal of employers to break strikes.

In order to secure the regime, Napoleon III wanted to prevent future Parisian revolts for all time. To this end, the emperor entrusted the task of remaking Paris to Baron Georges-Eugène Haussmann. Haussmann planned to turn Paris into an "'imperial capital' fit for the whole of Western civilization."[34] Haussmann's plans included a complete reshaping of Paris—street by street and building by building. As Walter Benjamin said, the true goal of Haussmann's plans was "to secure the city against civil war. He wanted to make the erection of barricades impossible for all time. . . . [He] seeks to neutralize these tactics on two fronts. Widening the streets is designed to make the erection of barricades impossible and new streets are to furnish the shortest route between the barracks and workers' districts. Contemporaries christen the operation 'strategic embellishment.'"[35]

Open spaces where crowds might congregate with seditious intent were done away with. Government buildings were made more secure from assault from insurgents. While Haussmann's reconstruction made Paris a city of glory, working-class districts remained slums.

A vast bureaucracy and administrative apparatus was now centered in Paris that Marx described as follows:

> This executive power with its enormous bureaucratic and military organization, with its extensive and artificial state machinery, with a host of officials numbering half a million, besides an army of another half million, this appalling parasitic body, which enmeshes the body of French society like a net and chokes all its pores . . . Every common interest was straightway severed from society, counterposed to it as a higher, general interest, snatched from the activity of society's members themselves and made an object of government activity, whether it was a bridge, a schoolhouse and the communal property of a village community, or the railways, the national wealth and the national university of France. Finally, in its struggle against the revolution, the parliamentary republic found itself compelled to strengthen, along with the repressive measures, the resources and centralization of governmental power.[36]

For Blanqui, the whole apparatus of the Second Empire was a monstrosity for oppressing the people that needed to be challenged and destroyed.

ESCAPE

In observing Napoleon III's success, Blanqui said in 1852 that it wasn't because he had the enthusiastic support of the people, rather: "Bonaparte has on his side only official or bought displays of support. On the other hand, he has against him only muted hostility from the various parties. No love, but no hatred either. He is no-one's total enemy."[37] Blanqui did not blame Napoleon III for the downfall of the Second Republic but condemned the failures of democracy: "It broke its promises of well-being and betrayed the people's hopes."[38] According to Blanqui, the people did not defend the Second Republic since it hadn't benefited them: "They compare the two regimes, and the comparison does not go in favor of democracy. Ultimately, the people only undertake revolutions in order to alleviate their suffering."[39] Now that the Second Republic was gone and the people passive, the bourgeoisie could rob France at will. Blanqui believed that there was no danger of a scandal exposing Bonaparte since the papers were compliant and extolled him: "Their government will not descend into scandal like that of Louis-Philippe. The gag guarantees them against this form of disaster. With her turpitude thus concealed, the goddess of lucre sits on her throne in complete safety, allowing seduced eyes to see nothing but her crown, glimmering with gold and precious stones."[40]

Blanqui saw little hope of the republican opposition being able to challenge the empire. Many were in now foreign exile fighting in petty feuds: "They box against each other atop the ruins, and wage a furious civil war between the various coteries. It is the most sublime ridiculousness. It seems that in London they squabble, they brawl over who is to make off with the bear's skin, while the bear itself freely makes a meal of the flock. What a fine pastime!"[41] Blanqui judged that Napoleon won't risk going to war since "it is a perilous game."[42] For the time being, Blanqui concluded that the Second Empire was stable.

When France allied with Britain and the Ottoman Empire against Russia in the Crimean War of 1854–1856, Blanqui refused to support it. He believed that the war threatened to end all opposition to Napoleon and that victory for France equaled one of tyranny.[43] By contrast, Barbès supported Napoleon and was pardoned by the

emperor. Even though Barbès protested his release and subsequent-
ly went into exile (where he would remain until his death in 1870),
his standing as a revolutionary was destroyed. As Marx noted, Barbès's release "decides the question as to who is the man of the Revolution and who not."[44]

Blanqui remained at Belle-Île for the next seven years. He suffered from many ailments in confinement, such as insomnia, diar-
rhea, and abdominal pains. The years of prison, isolation, and torture
were taking their toll on him. As Blanqui confessed to a follower,
he was "eaten up with boredom, anxiety, monotony and desponden-
cy, with days for ever like, with immobility, emptiness and nothing-
ness."[45] He wanted to return to the outside and raise the standard of
struggle once more. Blanqui did not intend to die alone in his cell.
For seven months, Blanqui worked on an elaborate plan with a fellow
inmate to escape by sea. On April 4, 1853, the two men were able to
make it outside the prison walls. The next day, they were recaptured,
returned to Belle-Île, and savagely beaten.

During his imprisonment in Doullens and Belle-Île, Blanqui
grew increasingly pessimistic about the possibilities for a revolutionary insurrection. Alan Spitzer observed that "in 1853, he wrote that
widespread prosperity under the Bonapartist regime rendered the
hopes for the chances of success or even the growth of a revolutionary party illusory."[46]

In 1857, he was moved to Corsica.[47] The following year, Blanqui
learned that his beloved mother Sophie passed away. On her deathbed,
she destroyed all Auguste's manuscripts in her possession to prevent
the police from discovering any incriminating evidence. It was Sophie's
final act of solidarity with her persecuted son.

Two more years were to pass in Napoleon's jails before his
sentence ended on April 2, 1859 (he was actually kept in jail until
August). The emperor followed the precedent set by Louis-Philippe
and kept Blanqui under police watch (and planned to deport him
to Cayenne in French Guiana). Despite Blanqui's pessimism on the
chances for revolution, he intended to resume his work. He said
of the current state of the French revolutionary left: "Fear has dissolved our army. . . . Isolated revolutionaries are still about, but not

a revolutionary party."[48] Returning to Paris, he sounded out those who "harbor the revolutionary idea in the depths of their hearts."[49] Blanqui did not think that economic conditions justified an insurrection, but he did encourage spreading socialist ideas through illegal newspapers that could serve as a spark to revive the class struggle.

Before Blanqui could begin the distribution of illegal propaganda, the police arrested him on March 10, 1861. According to the prosecution, "Blanqui has spent his life conspiring, he will continue to do so. He is dangerous to both society and to government. His presence in Paris cannot be tolerated. He must be put out of sight. . . . He has been in 1861 what he was in 1836."[50] Blanqui was charged with conspiracy, but the only evidence showed that he planned to spread underground propaganda. When Blanqui confronted the prosecutor, he did not ask for mercy but proclaimed that he was still at war:

> Prosecutor: This proves that despite twenty-five years in prison you have held the same ideas?
> Blanqui: Quite so.
> Prosecutor: Not only the same ideas, but to see their triumph?
> Blanqui: I shall desire it until death.[51]

It was a foregone conclusion that Blanqui would be convicted by the Second Empire. He was sentenced to four more years in prison (a decision which was upheld on appeal) and expected this next confinement would be his last. He wrote a final testament:

> My whole life I have fought for justice and right against iniquity and privilege, for the oppressed majority against an oppressing minority. I have been captive and poor; captive and poor I shall die. No one, I think, has a better right to say that the wretched are his brothers. It is difficult not to mingle pity for those who suffer with aversion for those who are the cause of the suffering. I have felt both compassion and rage; but I have harmed no one. I alone have paid for my indignation.[52]

Despite the best efforts of the government to keep things quiet, word of Blanqui's trial spread in France and abroad. To the public, the emperor appeared to be carrying out a vendetta against a single political opponent in violation of all legal norms. Marx said that

Blanqui's sentence was "one of the most outrageous that have ever been pronounced."[53]

Blanqui's latest place of incarceration was at Sainte-Pélagie, where he been locked up in 1832. Even though the food was horrible, the rules were not strict, and he was able to move about. He followed current events such as the US Civil War and took a pro-Union position.[54] He wrote a great deal and read Tacitus and Machiavelli's *Prince* (among other works). Bernstein observed that "with all his extensive reading, he neither got at the inside of events and movements nor saw them in their grand totality."[55]

At Sainte-Pélagie, Blanqui did not experience the same hatred from the other inmates as he had elsewhere. Many of the prisoners were devoted republicans who shared Blanqui's abiding hatred of the Second Empire. Students and intellectuals came to visit Blanqui, whom they considered a living legend. Some of these disciples were Georges Clemenceau (future leader of the Radical-Socialist Party and prime minister of France during World War I), Gustave Tridon, Eugène Protot, Paul Lafargue, and Charles Longuet (the latter two were future sons-in-law of Karl Marx and socialist politicians). Lafargue claimed years later, "Blanqui transformed us, corrupted us all. . . . To Blanqui falls the honor of having made the revolutionary education of a part of the youth of our generation."[56]

The nucleus of what would become the Blanquist party was born with these eager student converts. Their first common project was creation and distribution of the newspaper *Candide*, a radical atheist and republican journal.[57] *Candide* would not attack the regime directly, instead it challenged the spiritual arm of the Second Empire—the Catholic Church. After eight issues, *Candide* was suspended by the government for attacking the established faith.

By 1865, Blanqui's prison term was approaching its end, but that did not mean freedom. He was likely to be arrested once again on trumped-up charges or placed under heavy surveillance. Blanqui and his disciples decided to preempt that and planned his escape. On August 27, 1865, the plan went off without a hitch, and Blanqui left the country for Belgium.

Just a few scant years before, Blanqui had expected to die in prison. Now he had found a new lease on life. His new disciples were a sign of the rising opposition to the Second Empire. He planned to mold these eager revolutionaries into a disciplined organization capable of taking down Bonaparte.

VIII. THE DUTY
OF A REVOLUTIONARY

THE BLANQUIST PARTY

Now living in Belgium, Blanqui enjoyed his first taste of freedom in nearly thirty years. At sixty years of age, with white hair and shaky health, he could easily have retired from the struggle, but the revolutionary struggle beckoned him.

Still, it was going to take Blanqui time to create a new organization. For the first two years, according to Bernstein, his new party "was a group of propagandists bound together by a purpose and a tedious fidelity to their chief. It agitated among students and workers."[1] Blanqui sneaked into Paris every so often from his Belgian hideout to assist with the process of developing a new conspiratorial organization. Once, Lafargue warned Blanqui that he was exposing himself to unnecessary danger by staying in the capital. Blanqui replied with a smile, "I always carry my safe conduct with me," and took from his pocket copies of *Pays* and *Constitutionnel*. "If taken and searched, I will soon be freed when these Bonapartist and reactionary journals are found on me."[2]

The new party had a structure similar to the Society of Families and Seasons: pyramidal, secretive, and action-oriented. At most, the organization numbered 2,500 members.[3] However, the Blanquist

Party was much more tight-knit than even the Seasons. For example, copying down written orders was forbidden, and cell members knew only seven to ten other comrades at most (preventing anyone from compromising the organization). This had the desired effect: the organization was entirely free of police infiltration (specifics discussed below).

The Blanquist cadre was made up of professional revolutionaries, who were expected to be ready to take up arms at a moment's notice. There was a second layer to the organization of fellow travelers and sympathizers, who according to Patrick Hutton, "while occasionally willing to be demonstrative, were reluctant to be subversive.... [The Blanquist movement] is best described as two networks followers, each employing different methods, yet reinforcing one another in their common identification of the values of the revolutionary tradition with the legend of Blanqui."[4] In this group of sympathizers were Georges Clemenceau and Arthur Ranc.

The Blanquist movement was largely made up of workers, students, and intellectuals. The secretive nature of the Blanquist party has made it difficult for historians to determine their social composition. For instance, sources disagree on the numbers of workers in the party. Bernstein observes that while "several workers had already risen high in the party's high commanding posts ... [t]he available information shows that workers were a minority."[5] To the contrary, Spitzer argues that the majority of Blanqui's organization was drawn from the working class and that "the typical occupation of Blanquist workers captured in 1866 were cabinetmaker, carpenter, silversmith, etc."[6] One reliable indication of the party's composition comes from a list of forty-one Blanquists arrested on November 7, 1866. Sixteen of the Blanquists were artisans, and of that total, there were six woodworkers. In addition to the sixteen, there were six workers in commercial occupations. These two categories, totaling twenty-two, formed a bare majority of the arrested Blanquists. The next largest group included thirteen students (including six medical and four law students). Other Blanquists arrested included five professionals (a lawyer, "man of letters," and three journalists). Lastly, one man was classified as a shop owner.[7]

Due to its clandestine nature, the Blanquist party had difficulty reaching out to the workers. Blanqui urged his followers to "give more attention to the workers."[8] He was in favor of strikes, saying, "The strike is intelligible to every one; it is a simple idea, resistance to oppression. Everyone will rally to it."[9] According to Blanqui, since the strike was a "defense against capitalist oppression, the masses ought to concentrate all of their power toward political changes acknowledged as the only ones capable of implementing a social transformation and the just distribution of goods."[10] Still the disastrous experience of 1848 meant that Blanqui was reluctant to commit his organization to the struggle to day-to-day needs of workers.

The Blanquist understanding of the working class was still influenced by the experience of Jacobinism as the most oppressed class of the people. As Patrick Hutton argued, working-class members of the Blanquist party, such as Émile Duval, were "portrayed by his Blanquist comrades as the ideal type of worker—independent, resourceful, and energetic.... [They] conjured up a studied image of the ideal worker as a skilled professional with the independence of mind and resourcefulness to lead others."[11] Others, such as woodcutter Gustave Genton and railway engineer Edmond Megy, were valued by the Blanquists for their influence among French workers.

The ambivalence of the Blanquist approach toward the workers was reflected in their position toward the First International. The Blanquist party met sixteen times with members of the International in 1864 to establish a basis for joint cooperation, but they failed to establish a united front. Blanqui thought very little of the French section of the International, which was largely composed of Proudhonists. The Proudhonists took their inspiration from Pierre-Joseph Proudhon (1809–1865), a brilliant self-taught worker, who was one of the founding fathers of anarchism and author of the famous work *What Is Property?*, to which he answered: property is theft.[12] The Proudhonists believed that workers should refrain from political struggle and strikes. Instead, workers should establish a system of cooperatives and mutual aid. Proudhon's support for decentralization and local communes won support from workers who were opposed to the oppressive and bloated Bonapartist state. Blanqui believed these Proudhonist ideas to be harmful and a distraction from political struggle.

Marx himself shared Blanqui's hostility to Proudhonism and was eager to recruit the Blanquists into the International to counteract their influence. In 1865, Marx conveyed an invitation (via Paul Lafargue) for them to join.[13] The following year, the Blanquists took part in the International's Geneva Congress. The Geneva Congress was the high point of Proudhonist influence in the International, and resolutions were passed supporting mutualism, cooperation, and opposition to strikes.[14] Before the Congress, the Blanquists spread a story that the leaders of the Paris branch of the International were agents of the Bonapartist state. The bad blood generated by this rumor caused the International's General Council to recognize only the Proudhonists as the accredited delegation and disinvite the Blanquists. Blanqui sent a message to his men in Geneva, delivered by his trusted lieutenant Tridon, telling them to abstain from any further participation in the International. One member of the organization, Eugène Protot, disobeyed Blanqui's instructions. Protot spoke on the Congress floor, delivering polemical insults that caused physical fighting. The Blanquists were not going to ignore Protot's insubordination. When forty-one members of the party assembled at Le Café de la Renaissance in Paris on November 7, 1866, to review his offense, the police raided the meeting, taking all of them into custody.[15]

Despite the falling out between the Blanquists and the International, a few years later in 1869, Blanqui read Marx's devastating critique of Proudhon in the *Poverty of Philosophy*. Lafargue wrote to Marx in 1869, "Blanqui has a copy of it and lends it to all his friends. So Tridon read it, and was happy to see how il Moro [Marx] had disposed of Proudhon. Blanqui has the greatest respect for you. . . . He has found the best name I know for Proudhon; he calls him a hygrometer."[16] In a further irony, Proudhonist ideas were defeated at the International's Congresses at Brussels (1868) and Basle (1869) with the support of Marx. Still, Blanqui did not change his mind on the International.

STUDENTS AND INTELLECTUALS

By contrast, the Blanquists recruited some of their most dedicated and talented leaders from the students and the intellectuals. Those attracted to the Blanquist movement were generally convinced atheists. Religious questions among students in the Second Empire were bound to assume a political character, since as Patrick Hutton observed, "Louis-Napoléon's deference to high ecclesiastical officials in the shaping of educational policy was bound to promote a new wave of anticlericalism."[17] Opposition to religion in general, and the Catholic Church in particular, meant that the Blanquists found a ready audience among students interested in radical atheist propaganda.

The Blanquists were the driving force behind the Free Thought Movement, a radical atheist movement that tied the question of religion to politics. The Free Thought Movement first achieved prominence in October and November of 1865 at the International Student Congress held in Liège. The Congress was originally conceived as an international forum to discuss religious questions. The French delegation was composed largely of Blanquists, making the conference hostile to religion. The Blanquists set the radical and anti-religious tone for the Congress by covering the tricolor in black and marching around the hall to mourn for the death of academic freedom in France. The government and the Church were embarrassed by the student radicalism and quickly clamped down. Not only were students who participated in the Congress expelled from the university (one of whom was Paul Lafargue), anyone who showed open sympathy for them received the same treatment.[18]

The heavy-handed repression generated a student backlash. The students staged strikes, boycotts, and street demonstrations. According to Hutton, "the Blanquists watched these activities closely, abetted the agitation, and even staged a public banquet and demonstration on January 21, 1866, on the Rue des Amandiers in eastern Paris in the hope of rousing workers' support."[19] By the spring of 1866, the movement petered out when it became clear that the government would not accede to the students' demands to reinstate their expelled comrades.

By the late 1860s, the more liberal press and assembly laws provided for more space for the dissemination of radical atheism. Many Blanquist students and intellectuals worked as journalists to propagate the atheist cause. From 1865 to 1870, they founded or participated in a number of militant atheist journals such as *Candide, la Libre Pensée, la Nouvelle Pensée,* and *le Démocrite.* Among the journalists was the brilliant medical student, Dr. Albert Regnard, a participant at the Liège Congress and later a theoretician of the Blanquist movement.

LES HÉBERTISTES

Another Blanquist atheist intellectual was Gustave Tridon, the son of a wealthy landowner and heir to a large fortune (which he donated to the Blanquist movement). Tridon was noted for his sensitivity and for showing courage under fire (for example, when on trial for sedition in 1866). He was a prolific writer who touched on a wide range of political and philosophical topics.[20] Tridon was one of the chief theoreticians of the Blanquist movement, and according to Hutton, he "displayed a capacity for synthesis which Blanqui himself never acquired."[21] In 1864, Tridon wrote *Les Hébertistes,* a study of one of a radical movements of the French Revolution beloved by Blanqui.

Blanqui was attracted to Tridon's work not only because it portrayed the Hébertists as true revolutionaries but also because it highlighted their advocacy of science, atheism, and equality. *Les Hébertistes* hardened Blanqui's earlier opinion that Robespierre had betrayed the Hébertists and the French Revolution similarly to the neo-Jacobins in 1848. Both times, defenders of the lower orders had been betrayed by 'radicals' in power. According to Hutton, the crux of Tridon's argument was that Robespierre was "too removed from the people to sense their needs or emphasize with their plight. Unable to trust the popular will, Robespierre instituted the cult of the Supreme Being as a ruse to enforce civil disobedience. In this act, he revealed his hidden reactionary tendencies."[22]

Les Hébertistes also laid out a Blanquists ethical code, where the Hébertists were portrayed as full of "revolutionary virtue . . . to lead and yet be of the people."²³ According to Hutton, Tridon intended to set forth an atheistic consciousness, but, in actuality, he argued that "the capacity to lead in a revolutionary situation depended upon the depth of the leader's belief of the popular revolution. In matters of religion, faith had a liability; in matters of society, it was a decided asset."²⁴ Revolutionaries such as Hébert had infinite faith in the people and were willing to lead through heroic example. (No doubt Tridon saw Hébert as analogous to Blanqui.) Hutton writes, the days of revolution

> were popular festivals of rebirth. They signified a metamorphosis of illusion and reality in the sudden manifestation of the hidden consciousness of the people. The potential power of the 'damned of history' (the atheist pariahs who worked secretly for the intellectual liberation of mankind), which had seemed illusory to their enemies was revealed as real. The actual power of the reactionary forces who enjoyed privilege and position at the same time revealed as an illusion.²⁵

For Tridon, a revolution had a redemptive quality that allowed the people to escape darkness and oppression. When the last days of the revolution came in 1794 and the Hébertists were martyred, this showed that "revolutionary action was of value not only for its efficacy, but as a form of witness to the immortality of the revolutionary movement."²⁶ While the Hébertists had been defeated and become martyred for the cause, the Blanquists would take up their baton and carry it forward to victory. According to Blanqui's introduction to *Les Hébertistes*: "Let [the Hébertists'] tragic destiny be a teaching. They have failed and perished by the excess of passion. Devotion must not be delirium. But if it is good to avoid their defects, their qualities must serve as an example."²⁷

Tridon's acclamation of revolutionary martyrdom, sacrifice, and memory would become one of the hallmarks of Blanquist political culture. Hutton argues that for the Blanquists, "The courage to accept death for the revolutionary cause reaffirmed the tragic value of action. Its memory was important, for therein revolutionary energy was preserved for the future."²⁸

CIVIL BURIALS

To counteract the influence of the Catholic Church, the Blanquists developed their own rituals, rites, and festivals. One of the most important of these was the Civil Burial Movement that grew out of the Free Thought Movement. The Civil Burial Movement started as a mutual aid society, organized by Blanquists, to aid working-class families financially with funeral costs. It was hoped that civil burials would spare the poor and atheist workers from having to spend money on costly religious funerals. Civil burials were characterized by simple ceremonies and brief eulogies, as opposed to lavish religious burials. Through the culture of mutual aid and support they built up, civil burials became one of the main routes for the Blanquists to reach the working class.[29]

The Blanquists took on a number of pivotal roles in the Civil Burial Movement. Radical medical students provided free care for the needy. The Blanquist wine dealer Edmond Levraud hosted social events where wine was served alongside political discussions. A funeral Burial Society was organized and supported by the workers and Blanquist militants. Blanquists made sure to attend funerals of other members, which created bonds of solidarity between workers and militants.

RAOUL RIGAULT

Among the most faithful, incorruptible, and talented of the Blanquists was the young journalist Raoul Rigault (1846–1871). Rigault was a brilliant student but was expelled from the lycée at Versailles in 1866 for insubordination. Afterward, he frequented Bohemian cafés in the Latin Quarter, where he became known as an articulate advocate for a number of radical causes. Rigault was also a fanatical atheist and an admirer of Hébert. It wasn't long before he joined the Blanquist party. Rigault became an editor of the atheist journal, *le Démocrite* from 1868 to 1870 that was suppressed twice by the Imperial censorship and was shunned by moderates. While respectable opinion shunned Rigault, he "became a popular orator at public rallies . . . where he scandalized some listeners and titillated others with his attacks on marriage and family and his outspoken advocacy of free love."[30] Between 1868 and 1870, Rigault's speeches and actions against the Church and Empire led to twelve convictions.

After his first arrest in 1866, at Le Café de la Renaissance in Paris, Rigault developed a visceral hatred of the police and their spies. He was determined to study their methods and combat them. Rigault took it upon himself to develop a counterintelligence apparatus to free the Blanquist party from any police infiltration. He learned how to recognize police agents, "compiled lists of their names and addresses, ferreted out their frailties and peccadilloes, recorded their biographical details and the places where they frequented."[31] In disguise, Rigault followed agents provocateurs to court and carefully listened to their testimony of how they tracked their targets. Thanks to his careful and diligent work, the Blanquists not only had more detailed information on the police than the police had on them, but also, more importantly, they were kept free from spies. Blanqui praised Rigault's talents: "He is nothing but a gamin, but he makes a first-rate policeman."[32]

INSTRUCTIONS FOR AN ARMED UPRISING

After the Second Empire's liberalization in 1864, there was renewed activity by republicans and socialists, and waves of strikes by the workers. Blanqui and his followers believed these were signs the Empire was starting to fracture and that insurrection would soon be at hand. He made more frequent and longer trips to Paris, meeting his high command to review the organization and prepare for the great day. The belief that the day of judgment was approaching encouraged the Blanquists to step up their recruiting and open "centers of indoctrination, assembled weekly for inspection of ranks and considered the prerequisites of insurrection."[33] During this period, Blanqui codified his mature views on the art of insurrection and street fighting, drawing on nearly fifty years of experience. Blanqui's 1868 work, *Instructions for an Armed Uprising*, showed a master street fighter and revolutionary tactician at work, but it also revealed the fundamental weaknesses of his political and military strategy.

Many of Blanqui's ideas remained unchanged from the 1830s. The organization was centered in Paris by design (cells did exist outside the capital, but they were negligible). To Blanqui, it was only natural to focus the organization in the capital since Paris embodied the general will of France: "After all, the government of Paris is the government of the country by the country, thus the only legitimate one. Paris is not a municipal city confined to its own personal interests; it is a truly national representative."[34] If the revolution prevailed in Paris, the Blanquist party would be able to exercise its dictatorship over the country until the people were enlightened.

In his *Instructions*, Blanqui observed that the failure of previous Parisian uprisings was not due to a lack of spirit, but because "they lack organization. Without it, they haven't got a chance. Organization is victory; dispersion is death."[35] If revolutionaries possessed an organization, then they can win. Blanqui believed that his organization would provide the necessary cadre and officers to coordinate any future Parisian uprising and crown it with victory.

When weighing the respective forces at the command of the state and the revolution, the former had two advantages over the people: "breech-loading rifle and organization."[36] Blanqui observed that this strength was only relative because when government troops faced a well-organized insurrection, their morale would evaporate and they would go over to the side of the people. This would guarantee victory for the revolution. Blanqui said that the strength of the rebels comes not solely from organization, but from their devotion to an idea.

> There, they are all volunteers who are motivated by enthusiasm, not fear. They are superior to their adversary not only through devotion [dévouement], but even more so through intelligence. They have the moral and even the physical upper hand as a result of their conviction, vigour, and resourcefulness, their vitality of mind and body; they combine stout hearts with clear heads. No troops in the world are equal to these elite men.[37]

The power of the revolutionary idea must be channeled and disciplined by an organization if the people were going to prevail.

One of the central ingredients to the success of an insurrection was the construction of barricades. Blanqui believed that previous revolutions such as the June Days showed the dangers of disorganization in barricade construction where "each barricade has its particular group, more or less numerous, but always isolated. Whether it numbers ten or one hundred men, it does not maintain any communication with the other positions. Often there is not even a leader to direct the defense, and if there is, his influence is next to nil."[38] Due to the lack of structure among the insurgents, "defeat is certain" as the "enemy successively concentrates all his forces against one point, then on to a second, a third, a fourth, and thereby exterminates the insurrection one bit at a time."[39] Instead of leaving barricade construction to chance, Blanqui argued revolutionaries should plan their placement well before the uprising. To that end, *Instructions* provided an extended discussion on the proper ways to construct barricades.

The final victory of the revolution would come when the insurgents controlled the centers of political and repressive power. Once the revolutionaries had political power, they would establish their own Committee of Public Safety with the following tasks: "Thwart the maneuvers of the police and the counter-revolutionaries; to print, distribute and display the commander-in-chief's declarations or decrees; to maintain surveillance of the telegraphs, railways and all established centers of imperial power—in a word, to dismantle the enemy's means of action, and to organize and maintain those of the Republic."[40] In terms of dissolving the means of action of the enemy, Blanqui believed that it was necessary to completely disarm the army and the police. In their place, he advocated the general arming of the working class.

The *Instructions* were written as "purely military" and left "entirely to the side the political and social question," but in a number of unpublished works, Blanqui did list a series of political and economic measures that should be implemented.[41] According to Blanqui, the goal of the revolution was "for the benefit of labour against the tyranny of capital, and must reconstitute society on the basis of justice."[42] Once the Blanquists were in power, they needed to create a revolutionary dictatorship that would rule for an undetermined amount of time. Instead of repeating the mistakes of 1848, elections would be postponed until the population was enlightened. Debts would be abolished and a progressive income tax instituted. Capitalists would be instructed by the new state not to fire their workers, while those who disobeyed would have their assets seized and be exiled. Workers' assemblies would be organized to manage the economy. Blanqui claimed, "By commanding the bosses in this way, we will be able to parry the blows of capital, when it tries to stab us in the back."[43] Every action by the new order would deny freedom of movement for the enemy and create space for socialism to develop.

In the countryside, Blanqui believed that the "black army" of the Catholic Church ruled over the peasantry and kept them in darkness. To break the Church's hold, the revolutionaries had to deprive them of their privileges and control over education. The new state would institute free secular education to enlighten the peasantry. In handling the rural population, Bernstein writes that Blanqui "advised the utmost prudence with regard to the petty producers and peasants. Complete public ownership would not be decreed. It had to root itself slowly, by exhibiting its advantages to the small owner."[44] Blanqui was concerned not only with breaking the ideological hold of the Church but also gradually converting the peasants to new collective values.

In line with his earlier views, Blanqui recognized that "communism cannot impose itself suddenly, no more the day after than the day before its victory. To do so would be like attempting to fly to the sun."[45] After the revolution, a long period of transition lay ahead before universal education and association would finally succeed.

Blanqui's argument in *Instructions for an Armed Uprising*—that a conspiracy with clear leadership, strategy, and a program fired by revolutionary faith can overcome a superior adversary—possessed a fatal weakness: his plan did not involve any preparatory work among the workers. He simply assumed that on the day of the revolution, the masses would rally to the leadership of his organization. Blanqui left unanswered how the people were supposed to recognize the revolutionaries as their leaders. After all, a conspiracy can only be effective if it remains underground and secretive. If conspirators reach out to the masses to spread the revolutionary propaganda, they expose themselves to state repression.

Blanqui's focus on military matters harkened back to the 1830s, when it was reasonable to assume that the only option for revolutionaries was a secretive conspiracy. In those days, a mass movement of the working class in France was only just beginning to form. By 1848, that was no longer true. French workers had shown themselves able to conduct mass struggle without the aid of a conspiracy. During the Second Empire, the workers were challenging the regime in strikes and demonstrations. At no point did Blanqui discuss how to integrate working-class movement into his conception of revolution. His whole conception of politics left him unable to.

Blanqui's *Instructions for an Armed Uprising* laid down a set of fixed instructions for a revolutionary uprising that were supposed to be rigorously followed by insurgents. However, these rules did not take into account adaptations on the side of the bourgeois state, such as Haussmann's reforms that improved communications, developed railroads, and created wider streets to forestall barricade construction and enable the easy movement of troops and artillery. These reforms made Blanqui's plans and rules increasingly obsolete and future urban insurrections extremely difficult. The following century would see many revolutions and uprisings, but none were inspired by Blanqui's ideas. Blanqui's manual was not so much a harbinger of the future as it was an echo of a romantic revolutionary past.[46]

POSITIVISM AND VOLUNTARISM

The same year that Blanqui wrote his *Instructions for an Armed Uprising*, he also penned a series of critical notes on positivism. Positivism had emerged in the early nineteenth century, and one of the most well-known theorists was August Comte (1798–1857). Comte claimed society and history were governed by a series of scientific laws, and once they were understood, then society could be subjected to scientific management. The positivists posited a theory of progress and science that Blanqui rejected as fatalistic and dogmatic.

Blanqui did acknowledge the benefits of positivism, believing that it laid the intellectual foundations for atheism. He could only welcome that contribution of positivism. What was useful about positivism was its materialism, but once that was lost, then "nothing any more remains but errors and impertinence."[47] Since the positivists refused to take a clear stand defending the truths of materialism and atheism, they gave Christianity a free pass. To Blanqui, this was a sign that positivism was being "used as shelter for atheists and for shamefaced materialists who make a point of living in peace with the reigning force and never get mixed up with the radical movement."[48] By turning science away from materialism, the positivists not only undermined the truth of atheism, but retreated from challenging the existing order. For Blanqui, science and atheism were no ends in and of themselves but part and parcel of the revolutionary project.

According to Blanqui, positivism was not interested in challenging oppression; instead it used scientific theories to restructure society for the benefit of the privileged and the powerful. Once science is divorced from revolution, materialism, and enlightenment, then, he said, it can use scientific grounds to legitimize "all the atrocities of the victor." In addition, he stated, "Its long series of crimes are coldly transformed into a regular, inescapable evolution, like that of nature. . . . All that is, is legitimate, useful, essential. One must simply observe the natural procession of things, obligatory for mankind."[49] Ultimately, positivism is history and science preached from the vantage point of the oppressors. If the rule of the bourgeoisie was in line with progress, then the fate of the poor was something natural that they should accept. This, Blanqui could not and would not accept.

In contrast to the pseudo-progress preached by positivists, there was the real progress of communism that springs forth from science, equality, enlightenment, and association. Blanqui did not believe that progress would arrive of its own accord or followed a predetermined route. He rejected any fatalistic conception of progress: "I am not amongst those who claim that progress can be taken for granted, that humanity cannot go backwards. . . . No, there is no fatality, otherwise the history of humanity, which is written hour by hour, would be entirely written in advance."[50] According to Geffroy: "Blanqui placed at a crossroads of revolution the clear and appealing lag of his uncertainty."[51] The possibilities were open for either the advance to communism or the regression into slavery. Progress and the success of communism depended on the revolution and in the last instance, depended upon the will of a dedicated few. Walter Benjamin said that Blanqui's politics hinged on this:

> The activities of a professional conspirator like Blanqui certainly do not presuppose any belief in progress—they merely presuppose a determination to do away with present injustice. The firm resolve to snatch humanity at the last moment from the catastrophe looming at every turn is characteristic of Blanqui—more so than of any other revolutionary politician of the time. He always refused to develop plans for what comes "later."[52]

The revolutionary effort, the will to fight and to win against insurmountable odds, can unveil unseen roads to communism. And these roads are not given to anyone in advance but are revealed in the course of struggle. Blanqui was not oblivious to the obstacles confronting revolutionaries but believed these could be surmounted by an act of will and unbreakable faith in an idea. As he said:

> Revolutions desire men who have faith in them. To doubt their triumphs is to already betray them. It is through logic and audacity that one launches them and saves them. If you lack these qualities, your enemies will have it over you; they will only see one thing in your weaknesses—the measure of their own forces. And their courage will grow in direct proportion with your timidity.[53]

Blanqui's ethic is if you lack the will to win or hesitate in carrying out what the revolution demands of you, not only will you lose to the enemy, but you are also a traitor to the cause you claim to serve.

In contrast to the positivists, Blanqui believed that science and atheism must not be divorced from the revolution and the liberation of the people. To do so was to create a theory of progress that justified the existing order and condemned all forms of rebellions. While Blanqui believed communism was truly in line with progress and science, it could not be realized on its own. To realize the radiant future required the conscious intervention of a revolutionary elite through an act of will. Blanqui summed his voluntaristic doctrine with the following imperative: "The duty of a revolutionary is always to struggle, to struggle no matter what, to struggle to extinction."[54]

AUGUST 14

The rising labor militancy of 1860s was undermining the Second Empire's ability to rule. In 1867, Haussmann was dismissed in the wake of a financial scandal. The opposition, whether republican, Internationalist, or Blanquist, was holding open demonstrations and defying the police. To suppress it with armed force was to court revolution.

To restore his prestige, the emperor ordered a plebiscite to ask the voters whether they approved the liberal constitution. On May 8, 1870, the constitution was approved by 7.3 million votes against 1.5 million, with 1.8 million abstentions. The opposition (which could not decide whether to boycott or partake in the plebiscite) was defeated in Paris, receiving only 45,000 votes out of an electorate of 323,000. The dynasty received substantial support from the countryside in the face of the red menace. More troubling for Napoleon was that 15 percent of the army—15,000 soldiers—voted against the Empire.

In January 1870, the regime was shaken by news that Prince Pierre Bonaparte had killed the journalist Victor Noir, columnist of *La Marseillaise* (which included both Blanquists and Internationalists among its contributors), edited by the republican Henri Rochefort. Public anger was shown when more than 200,000 turned out in the pouring rain for Noir's funeral. The government was prepared for a clash and readied 60,000 soldiers to prevent an insurrection.

Armed Blanquists were in the procession and, unbeknown to them, Blanqui reviewed them from afar at the Champs-Élysées:

> He recognized the squadron leaders, as they came into view, and, behind each of them, he saw the men grouped geometrically and marching in step, as though in regiments. It was all done according to plan. Blanqui held his review-strange spectacle without arousing the slightest suspicion. Leaning against a tree, surrounded by the crowd of

onlookers, the vigilant old man saw his comrades pass by, orderly amid the surging of the people, silent amid the steadily mounting uproar.[55]

The police were angered over the political nature of the funeral and arrested known subversives on charges of conspiracy.

Several days later, Rochefort was arrested for saying, "My error has been to believe that a Bonaparte could be other than an assassin." This nearly provoked a general insurrection. Barricades were erected in Paris for the first time in nearly two decades and 300 were arrested. In April, the government unmasked a vast "plot" to kill the emperor, providing a convenient pretext to arrest over 450 left-wing leaders (380 were later released for lack of evidence).[56]

At the same time as the Rochefort events, workers struck at le Creusot steelworks. The strike was initially settled, but the embers flared up again in March and April. The strike became violent, with soldiers shooting down the workers. The strike was also noted for the fierce fighting between women and the gendarmes. The authorities were not supported by the populace; rather there were protests and agitation in support of the workers.

When Napoleon III assumed the throne, he declared that "the era of revolution was over." Now the specter of revolution was haunting France once more. Economic stagnation, militant class struggle, and deteriorating living standards had all served to bring France to the brink. The emperor planned to unite the country behind the throne once more by rallying the populace to the flag and defense of the homeland in a war. War with Prussia was the only way out.

By 1870, tensions were at the breaking point between France and Prussia. A minor diplomatic incident over who was going to inherit the Spanish throne proved to be the pretext. On July 19, 1870, France declared war on Prussia.

The declaration of war activated Prussia's alliances with other German states. The German army was well led and well equipped, with more than a half-million men at its disposal and experienced from its recent conflicts fighting for German unification. By contrast, the French army of approximately 300,000 was, according to Frank Jellinek, "as hollow and corrupt as the Empire it served."[57] Profiteering reached scandalous proportions among the officer corps. The leaders of the army had not kept up with new theories of war and remained inflexible in their thinking. In the field, the French army suffered continual defeats. Rank-and-file troops stationed around Paris were considered unreliable. The Empire did not arm the male population due to fears of what would happen once the workers had guns.

The Blanquists believed the time had finally come to launch their coup. Blanqui was summoned back to France by two of his commanders, Émile Eudes and Ernest Granger. They argued that an insurrection could take advantage of popular discontent and warned that "the conspiracy had already lost a majority of its adherents through its inaction and that a further postponement of the coup which was its raison d'être would alienate the enthusiasts who remained."[58] While the two men argued for immediate action, Blanqui was much more cautious about their chances. He believed that the organization lacked the men necessary to win, that an uprising was premature, and without support from the workers they would fail. On August 13, the proponents of action carried the day, and Blanqui was outvoted.

The next day, Blanqui ordered 400 men, armed with 300 revolvers and 400 daggers, to assault the barracks of La Villette.[59] Blanqui appealed to the soldiers to join the insurrection and turn over their arms to the populace. They refused. Then the Blanquists moved into the working-class district of Belleville, shouting revolutionary slogans in order to rally the people. The populace was completely unresponsive, and Blanqui ordered his men to disperse. Imperial soldiers hadn't even arrived. Blanqui provided his own account as to what went wrong:

> The population appeared dumbstruck. Attracted by curiosity, but held back by fear, they stood immobile and silent, backed up against the houses. The boulevard that the insurgents were on was completely deserted. In vain did they appeal to the onlookers by shouting, "Long live the Republic! Death to the Prussians! To arms!" Not a word, not a gesture was given in response to this agitation. . . . The fact is, in this very revolutionary district of Belleville, the uprising did not attract a single recruit. . . . We have no guns and as you see no one will join us. We can do nothing without the people![60]

After years of organizing and planning, Blanqui's expected revolutionary coup ended in an utter fiasco. Despite his best efforts, a revolution could not be willed into existence nor could it be accomplished without the people.

Eudes and Gabriel-Marie Brideau were arrested shortly afterward and sentenced to death. Influential figures begged for mercy and insisted that rebels had acted out of a misguided sense of patriotism. This succeeded and their punishment was commuted.

A mere few weeks later on September 2, the French Army was decisively defeated at the Battle of Sedan and the emperor captured by the Prussians. Two days later, popular pressure in Paris led to the creation of the Third Republic. The Second Empire was swept aside with nary a tear being shed.

IX. War and Revolution

La Patrie en Danger

On September 7, just three days after the formation of the Third Republic, Blanqui founded a newspaper, *La Patrie en Danger*. Blanqui's paper reflected the nationalist mood in Paris on the need to defend France from German subjugation. While Blanqui and other radicals had condemned the war with Prussia when Napoleon III was in power, now they believed its character had changed. Initially, the war was a defensive one on the part of Germany against French aggression but had transformed into one of conquest and occupation. According to Marx: "The war of defense ended, in point of fact, with the surrender of Louis Bonaparte, the Sedan capitulation, and the proclamation of the republic at Paris. But long before these events, the very moment that the utter rottenness of the imperialist arms became evident, the Prussian military camarilla had resolved upon conquest."[1]

The International's French section revived by mobilizing the people of Paris to defend the Republic. To accomplish this, the International organized committees of public safety similar to the Jacobins.[2] The Parisian section demanded that the Third Republic truly break with the repressive laws of the Second Empire by arming the National Guard and enacting policies to advance the interests of workers. The radicals' desire for a vigorous defense of France ran against the inclinations of the new republican government, who were more fearful of mobilizing the Parisian population and the prospect of a social revolution than of the Prussians at the gates. In time, this fear grew so large that the Third Republic was willing to utilize German troops to crush the Parisian populace. All this fed into a broad distrust of the government among the working class, who saw the Republic as in league with Germany and treasonous to the interests of both the French nation and the people.

In line with other radicals, Blanqui argued that only a levée en masse like the Jacobins raised during the First Republic could defeat Prussia. Blanqui's paper revived the old revolutionary calendar, no doubt, as Bernstein argues "to remind the governing contemporaries that their ancestors had saved the Republic from demolition and the country from dismemberment."[3] Blanqui gave his full support to the French government in the face of the German invader, putting aside any talk of class struggle: "Do not forget that to-morrow we are going to fight, not for a government, not for interests of caste or party, not even for honor, principles or ideas, but for what is the life and breath of all, for that which constitutes humanity in its most noble manifestation, for country."[4]

Blanqui's patriotism was no aberration. He had long believed that France had a special destiny as the world leader of revolution. This special role was reserved for France because the country possessed "a dynamic spirit [which] had already destroyed its own moribund traditions and contributed so greatly to the liberation of other peoples, [and] was the bearer of [the] 'principle of equality' destined to conquer the nations."[5] What mattered for the success of the world revolution was not international events but the situation in France. Blanqui believed that if France was ruled by revolutionaries, then it would be a signal for the liberation of the workers across the world. On the other hand, if France was ruled by monarchs or bourgeois reactionaries, then the world revolution could not advance.

The French revolutionary tradition, whether Jacobin, Hébertist, Babouvist, or Carbonari, determined his tactics, strategy, and view of history. Blanqui believed that the French people in general and the workers in particular were the true heirs to that tradition. Part of Blanqui's objection to the Bourbons was that they were foreigners and not representative of the real France. The real France was that of popular sovereignty, a republic, and equality.

Blanqui was not a narrow nationalist. He did not support France's war in the Crimea or any other foreign adventures of Napoleon III. He was widely read and was sympathetic to foreign socialists who were dedicated revolutionaries (such as Marx). While Blanqui was not above the racist prejudices of his time (stating that whites were likely more intelligent than blacks), at other times he did condemn British colonialism and white supremacy.[6] At one point in his writings, Blanqui identified the workers of all countries as possessing the same interests and the same enemies:

> Workers of all nations are brothers, and they have only one enemy: the oppressor who forces them to kill each other on the battlefields.
>
> Everyone, workers and peasants of France, Germany or England, of Europe, Asia or America—everyone, all of us have the same toils, the same forms of suffering, the same interests. What do we have in common with this race of gilded idlers who are not content to live merely from our sweat but who also want to drink our blood?[7]

In September 1870, like many other French radicals, his nationalism overrode his socialist principles. For Blanqui, the character of the war changed once France had a republic: now it was waging a defensive war against an authoritarian foe. How could Frenchmen fight one another when an enemy was standing in their doorway? Blanqui declared in the September 6 issue of *La Patrie en Danger*: "No more parties or shadings . . . The government that has emerged . . . represents the thinking of the people and the national defense. That is enough. All opposition, all contradiction must disappear before the common warfare."[8] Edward Mason says that Blanqui's writings in *La Patrie en Danger* descended into some of the lowest forms of chauvinism: "He stigmatized the German invaders as 'Vandals,' 'Goths,' 'barbarians' in a manner which would have done credit to 1914."[9] While Blanqui's columns reeked of chauvinism, these views were shared across the far left, who believed it was imperative to defend the 'revolutionary nation' of France from the onslaught of 'Prussian barbarism.'

Blanqui formed a club with the same name as his paper, *La Patrie en Danger*. Both the paper and club were largely devoid of discussions on divisive topics such as politics and class struggle. Blanqui's overriding concern was on military affairs: where the enemy was coming from, how to outmaneuver them, and how to defend France. In the face of besieged Paris, Blanqui believed that the population should be armed and "demanded the fullest production of war goods . . . the building of barricades, the nationalization of all necessities, the dismissal of Bonapartist civil servants and a set of measures that would put the country on a firm war-footing."[10] Even though Blanqui had disavowed the heritage of Robespierre and the Jacobins, he was calling for a return to the policies of Year II that had saved the First Republic.[11] The country was in danger and only emergency measures could save it. Blanqui knew that in order for the Jacobins to implement their policies, they had to overthrow the moderate Girondins first. Despite *La Patrie en Danger*'s small audience, this warning was not lost upon the leaders of the Third Republic.

OCTOBER 31

The Government of National Defense that took over on September 4 had little intention of waging the type of revolutionary war that Blanqui wanted. This was a decidedly conservative body that was more interested in preserving property and forestalling revolution than in fighting the Prussians. These politics were reflected in the leaders who now made up the Third Republic, who ranged from moderate republicans to royalists. The new president was General Louis-Jules Trochu, who had been the military governor of Paris under Napoleon III. While Trochu was an Orleanist, he was willing to work with the republican bourgeoisie to maintain order. The vice-president and minister of foreign affairs was Jules Favre. Favre was a conservative republican who during the Second Republic had censored newspaper articles that attacked private property and ordered the deportation without trial of the June insurgents. Two other government ministers, Jules Simon and Jules Ferry, opposed any legislative measures to reduce economic inequality. The democratic radical Leon Gambetta was the minister of the interior, who appealed for national unity and an all-out war against Prussia. In February 1871, Gambetta would oppose the armistice with Prussia and be forced to resign. One radical, Henri Rochefort, was co-opted to serve as a minister without portfolio in the government.

The chief diplomat of the Government of National Defense was Adolphe Thiers, who later became president of the Third Republic. Thiers had a long career in service to every French government since the 1830s. Under the Orleanist dynasty, he was the minister of the interior (and later the prime minister) where he had ordered the suppression of the Parisian uprising of 1834. Thiers had helped bring down the Second Republic by assisting Louis Bonaparte's rise to power. Even though Thiers was an early advocate of war against Prussia, once he realized it was lost, he became an advocate for peace. Through careful political maneuvering, Thiers managed to distance himself from the Government of National Defense when the armistice was signed in February 1871. That same month, he was elected chief executive of the republic. In that position, Thiers orchestrated the suppression of the Paris Commune at the end of May 1871.[12]

Despite making the transition from empire to republic, very little had changed. The bureaucracy and leading men were holdovers from previous regimes. While many members of the government wanted to continue fighting Prussia, the situation was becoming hopeless. General Trochu and the high command were convinced that most of the French army "were unfit for action, being poorly trained and poorly disciplined."[13] The Prussians had not only crushed the French army in a little under a month, but by September 19, they had surrounded Paris, cutting off supplies and communications. Paris was prepared to withstand a siege with a strengthening of its defensive positions and equipping by enrolling most of the able-bodied men into the National Guard. Patriotic feeling was inflamed as the Parisians prepared to fight street to street when the Prussians stormed the city. Instead, the Germans simply surrounded the city, planning to starve it into submission.

While official pronouncements were bellicose, the government was sending out diplomats such as Thiers to arrange an armistice with Germany. Bismarck was demanding a large indemnity and the cession of the provinces of Alsace-Lorraine. This threatened the very integrity of the Republic. As news of the Government of National Defense's half-hearted conduct of the war effort leaked, revolutionaries and patriots were enraged and accused the government of treason. Blanqui said, "Are men who are certain of defeat disposed to fight? What is the good of organizing a defense considered useless and powerless in advance?"[14]

Blanqui had raised doubts as to the government's commitment to defense early in September, but by October he was calling members of the government "unscrupulous" and "lackeys of Bonaparte." When the government called for elections to a National Assembly, Blanqui believed that this was a prelude to surrender. According to Bernstein, he insisted "that all males in Paris who bore arms should elect a committee of nine men, a sort of Committee of Public Safety (although he did not use that name) which, invested with dictatorial power, would continue to wage war until the enemy was annihilated."[15] Blanqui repeated his call for a levée en masse and sacrifices by every Frenchmen in an all-out struggle against Prussia. His proposals received support in both Paris and the National Guard.

On October 28, news reached Paris that the fortress of Metz with its 150,000 men had surrendered, the village Le Bourget was captured, and armistice negotiations had failed. The population was enraged and believed that treason was responsible for all these setbacks. On October 31, a crowd of several thousand patriots and National Guardsmen gathered outside of the Hôtel de Ville. They denounced armistice negotiations and called for renewed resistance and the establishment of a commune. The crowd refused to be placated and arrested members of the government.

A new revolutionary provisional government was proclaimed consisting of fourteen names including Victor Hugo, Louis Blanc, Gustave Flourens, and Blanqui. Blanqui had not taken part in the demonstration, but he answered the call to leadership. He made his way to the Hôtel de Ville, where he effectively served as the new minister of the interior. Blanqui began by issuing proclamations, one of which read: "The population of Paris has judged it necessary to replace the government which has compromised the Republic."[16] Blanqui's decrees were designed to strengthen the city from internal and external enemies. He also appointed Raoul Rigault as the new prefect of the police.

The revolutionaries did not have support from the bulk of the National Guard or other left-wing groups such as the International-ists or the Proudhonists. The Government of National Defense was able to muster loyalist members of the National Guard, who con-vinced the revolutionaries to leave. The government promised new elections and that there would be no reprisals against the far left.[17] These pledges were violated almost immediately when twenty-two leftist leaders were arrested and sixteen members of the National Guard were dismissed. Blanqui, who had been elected commander of the 169th battalion of the National Guard a month before with support from Clemenceau, was removed. The anti-radical General Clément-Thomas was appointed to head the National Guard. Blan-qui was forced to go into hiding.

Days later, the Government of National Defense held a plebi-scite and municipal elections in Paris to determine if the population supported them. The result was a victory for the government with 557,900 yes votes against 65,000 no votes and 300,000 abstentions. In the municipal elections, the revolutionary left elected mayors and assistant mayors.[18] The left was shown to be a minority force among Parisian workers, and the government took that as a mandate to suppress all opposition. Still, Parisian population remained deter-mined to resist the Prussians and viewed the government as defeatist. Blanqui gave voice to the boiling tensions: "Legitimate power now belongs to those who are determined to resist. The real voting ballot papers, today, are bullets."[19]

THE LAST WORD

While Blanqui was in hiding, he continued to assail the government in *La Patrie en Danger*. He condemned calls for elections to a new Constituent Assembly as distracting from the defense of Paris. Still, the paper's readership dropped and expenses rose. On December 8, *La Patrie en Danger* was forced to suspend publication.

The revolutionary temperature in Paris continued to rise. As winter set in, starvation and unemployment coupled with military setbacks had turned large swaths of the Parisian population against the Government of National Defense. Even though the government no longer believed that it was possible to defeat Prussia, they still felt obligated to make promises of victory in order to appease public opinion. In contrast to the rest of France, the Parisians not only remained unbroken but demanded even more energetic and revolutionary measures to win the war. As Robert Tombs said, "The French and Prussian governments faced the same problem: how could the Parisians be induced to accept defeat?"[20]

On January 5, Bismarck began heavy bombardment of Paris to subdue the population. This had the opposite result, and the determination of the Parisians was only reinforced. On January 6, delegations from twenty arrondissements issued "The Red Poster" that criticized the government for being "preoccupied with negotiating instead of manufacturing artillery and armaments. They have refused an all-out offensive mobilization. They have left Bonapartists in place and thrown republicans into prison. . . . In spite of their having at their disposal all necessary resources, supplies and men, they have been incapable of both administration and fighting."[21]

The government responded by arresting some of the signatories. They also planned an attack on the Prussians that they hoped would serve as a bloodletting for the National Guard and finally prove there was no chance of military victory.

On January 19, 90,000 French soldiers, including 40,000 National Guardsmen launched a massive offensive against the Germans that quickly came to a standstill amidst general confusion and panic. The French suffered more than 4,000 casualties, while the Germans lost only 600 men. As a result of the disaster, Trochu was replaced as military governor of Paris by the reactionary General Vinoy. The Blanquists and other leftists believed that the defeat of the January 19 attack was due to sabotage.[22] The resulting failure only raised popular anger against the government to a fever pitch. Sections of the government, particularly those surrounding Thiers, looked approvingly on the German army for "disciplining" the Parisian masses.

The Blanquists Théodore Sapia, Édouard Vaillant, Émile Leverdays, Théophile Ferré, and Tridon planned a new insurrection in coordination with the leaders of the National Guard. On the night of January 21, a crowd invaded the prison of Mazas to free Flourens and other participants in the October 31 coup. When Blanqui was approached by his comrades the next day to take charge of the insurrection, he refused. He believed that the whole endeavor was foolhardy. Instead, Blanqui retired to a nearby café to watch events unfold. By mid-day on January 22, a few hundred protesters and Blanquists in National Guard units from the 13th, 14th, and 17th arrondissements had gathered outside the Hôtel de Ville. This time, the government had stationed marines and troops inside. These soldiers fired upon the insurgents, sparking a brief battle. When it was all over, Sapia (a Blanquist) and six National Guardsmen lay dead and eighteen civilians were wounded.[23]

In response to the insurrection, the Government of National Defense launched another wave of repression against the left: radical clubs were closed, newspapers shut down, and eighty-three were arrested. Jules Favre said in retrospect that "the January 22 uprising had been no full-scale attempt at revolution . . . But the shooting changed everything, and Paris hardened into two irreconcilable camps."[24] A further blow to Paris was a January 28th announcement that France had agreed to an armistice with Germany. The terms of the armistice provided for an election of a National Assembly to ratify terms, the surrender of northern and eastern Parisian forts, the payment of an indemnity of 200 million francs within a fortnight, and the disarmament of regular troops (the National Guard was permitted to keep their arms).

The elections on February 8 brought a sweeping victory to royalists throughout the countryside. The new National Assembly embodied two ideas: monarchy and peace. On February 12, an exhausted and demoralized Blanqui left Paris for Bordeaux to recuperate. That same day, he wrote the pamphlet *Un Dernier Mot*, denouncing the government's capitulation. He said, "The dictatorship of the Hôtel de Ville stands accused, therefore, of high treason, and of launching an assault upon the very existence of the nation."[25] At the home of an old friend, Dr. Lacambre, in the Department of Lot, he learned that a court-martial had condemned him to death for his role on October 31. On March 17, Blanqui was finally caught and imprisoned in Figeac. Two months later, he was transferred to the prison of Château du Taureau, near Morlaix. The day after Blanqui's capture, the National Guard rose up in Paris, beginning the Commune. In a cruel twist of fate, Blanqui missed the revolution that he had struggled for decades to achieve.

Road to Revolution

Paris was at the center of the revolutionary maelstrom that engulfed France from 1870 to 1871. The intense class struggles and the emergence of a revolutionary left that marked the closing days of the Second Empire carried over to the Third Republic. Social strife was escalated due to the economic and political disruption caused by the Franco-Prussian War, which was even further aggravated by defeat. To the workers, the leaders of the Third Republic were seen as responsible for France's military defeat and beholden to wealthy capitalists and monarchists. During the long drawn-out Prussian siege, Paris endured starvation and suffering that further widened the gulf between the classes. Gradually, the idea of a revolutionary Commune took root among Parisians as the only viable political alternative to the bourgeois Republic. The rise of a mass National Guard, political clubs, and vigilance committees posed an alternative to the existing order that came to fruition with the formation of the Paris Commune.

It is necessary here to pause and discuss the role of the National Guard. Following the defeat at Sedan that left of the most of the French Army captured, the National Guard was the only organized force capable of defending Paris. The Third Republic was frightened by this democratic armed force based among the workers. The National Guard was different from normal armies, with their elitist and hierarchical ethos. All officers of the National Guard were elected (except for the government-appointed commander-in-chief) and subject to recall (allowing the battalions to reflect the ever-changing popular mood). While revolutionary influence was limited in the National Guard, workers were already suspicious and hostile to the government due to its greater fear of the armed workers than of the Prussians. By March 1871, the National Guard had 340,000 members, almost the whole of the able-bodied male population of Paris.

Government worries about the National Guard and Paris were not completely unfounded. After the creation of the Third Republic, both republicans and socialists (in the ranks of both the Internationalists and the Blanquists) wanted to mobilize the population for all-out war, which they believed by force of circumstances would unleash revolutionary measures and bring a far left government to power, as occurred with the Jacobins in 1793. This was precisely the type of situation that the Government of National Defense wished to avoid by ending the war quickly and taking swift steps to prevent social revolution.

The left's ideas for a new government and revolutionary defense were summarized in a poster that was put up by the Central Committee of the Twenty Arrondisements on September 15, 1870. The Central Committee outlined the conditions for "a truly republican regime, calling upon the permanent participation of individual initiative and popular solidarity."[26] Its program called for democratization of existing social, political, and economic structures; and the abolition of the police, bureaucracy, and judiciary. The defense of Paris was to be left to the National Guard, in which "the people shall have powers of supervision over all defense operations."[27] The National Guard would also be responsible for requisitioning and rationing. Such energetic actions, it was believed, would safeguard popular control over the Republic and the war effort. The vigorous measures the left demanded were not forthcoming from the government.

Government hostility was compounded by the desperate siege conditions in Paris. The Prussian blockade had cut off food supplies, completely ruined the economy, and brought wide-scale unemployment for most of the middle class. Furthermore, the government did little to organize relief efforts since they were hampered by their belief in the principles of economic freedom and, according to Robert Tombs, they were "reluctant to cause public alarm or provoke the disappearance of food stocks underground into a black market. So it introduced a bare minimum of requisitioning and rationing. Policy was incoherent and less than efficient. Requisitions and controls were brought in piecemeal, often too late."[28] The burden of shortages, price rises, and long queues fell heaviest on working-class families (particularly women).[29] During the siege, speculators amassed enormous profits, which only made the populace more receptive to revolutionary demands for price controls and social justice.

Throughout the winter of 1870–71, conditions in Paris deteriorated even further as temperatures dropped to subzero levels. During Christmas, while people in working-class neighborhoods were dying of starvation, the wealthy districts and restaurants held festive celebrations with plenty of food. The Germans made sure Paris was reminded of war by periodical bombardments. By the time the Prussians lifted the siege in March, it was estimated that there were 64,154 deaths. According to Donny Gluckstein, "Workers suffered disproportionately, their death rate being twice that of the upper class."[30] The Republic maintained the National Guard out of necessity, and despite the low pay for Guardsmen, employment in the Guard for families could mean the difference between food on the table or starvation. As the siege progressed, more than 900,000 people became dependent in one form or another on the National Guard.

As conditions grew worse, the idea of the Commune took root as not simply municipal power but as an alternative polity. To the people of Paris, the Commune would solve inequality, starvation, and government treason by placing power in the hands of the people. As Marx said, "The cry of 'Social Republic,' with which the revolution of February was ushered in by the Paris proletariat, did but express a vague aspiration after a Republic that was not only to supersede the monarchical form of class-rule, but class-rule itself. The Commune was the positive form of that Republic."[31]

In January, the Republic concluded an armistice, which not only cost the country a large indemnity (to be paid on the backs of the workers), but also surrendered the provinces of Alsace-Lorraine to the Germans. In February, elections to the National Assembly returned a monarchist majority who proceeded to approve the armistice terms by a vote of 546 to 107. Paris was outraged by the armistice and the election results. They had suffered heavily in the war, only to see the Republic prostrate itself before the invaders instead of rallying the people in arms to fight. The elections also raised the specter of a royalist restoration feared by a red and republican Paris.

In a further blow to national pride, the National Assembly permitted the Germans to parade 30,000 troops through the capital on March 1. The National Guard called for continued resistance to the Germans and reorganized themselves by electing a Central Committee. Massive patriotic demonstrations were held on February 24 to mark the anniversary of 1848 revolution. Parisians seized arms and ammunition to prepare for a final battle with the Germans. However, the First International, Vigilance Committees, and other popular groups in Paris warned the National Guard against provoking any confrontation with the Prussians. Eventually, the Central Committee relented, and the popular organizations decided to passively boycott the Germans. Communard participant and historian Pierre-Olivier Lissagaray described how Germans were greeted when they entered Paris:

> They were assailed only by the gibes of guttersnipes. The statues on the Place de la Concorde were veiled in black. Not a shop or café was open. No one spoke to them. A silent, mournful crowd glowered at them as if they had been a pest of vermin. A few barbarian officers were permitted a hasty visit to the Louvre. They were isolated as if they had been lepers. When they glumly retired, on March 3, a great bonfire was kindled at the Arc de Triomphe to purify the soil fouled by the invader's tread. A few prostitutes who had consorted with Prussian officers were beaten, and a café which had opened its doors was wrecked. The Central Committee had united all Paris in a great moral victory; even more, it had united it against the government which had inflicted this humiliation.[32]

Before France signed the treaty, the National Guard and the revolutionaries in Paris were caught in a bind over how to back the war effort without also supporting the government. After the peace treaty was an accomplished fact, that problem was gone, and nothing remained to distract the Parisians from confronting the government.

The National Assembly passed two provocative and vindictive decrees that brought antagonisms in Paris to the boiling point. First, the National Assembly moved to Versailles, fearing the insurrectionary mood in Paris. To all Parisians, this was a blow to the prestige of the capital. Secondly, during the war there had been a moratorium on debt repayment, which the National Assembly lifted on March 13. This struck hard both the impoverished working class and small shopkeepers. Lissagaray describes the impact: "Two or three hundred thousand workmen, shopkeepers, model makers, small manufacturers working in their own lodgings, who had spent their little stock of money and could not yet earn any more, all business being at a standstill, were thus thrown upon the tender mercies of the landlord, of hunger and bankruptcy."[33] Now the broad masses of Paris were united against the government in Versailles.

Disorder continued to rise in Paris, frightening the bourgeoisie and causing approximately 100,000 of them to leave before the revolution. The National Guard was no longer under government control, since their newly appointed commander-in-chief was viewed as a royalist and a defeatist.[34] Versailles saw the National Guard was now a threat to their authority, property, and social order. The National Assembly wanted to preserve order in the capital, but had only 12,000 regular soldiers under its command. Thiers wanted the Guard disarmed but had to move carefully to avoid provoking an armed confrontation.

On March 18, Thiers sent troops into Paris to retake 400 cannons under National Guard control. For the Guard, these guns were symbols of the independent power of Paris and its revolutionary people.[35] Initially, everything went according to plan and the soldiers seized the cannons. However, no one thought to bring horses to carry away the heavy weapons. So the soldiers waited, but word spread across Paris that they were being disarmed. The population gathered around the soldiers—who were miserable, demoralized, and tired of war. The troops fraternized with the crowd and arrested their commanders.[36] After the mutiny, Generals Claude Martin Lecomte and Jacques Léonard Clément-Thomas were executed by their own men (despite efforts by the National Guard to prevent the executions). Those soldiers who did not join the revolutionary crowd escaped from the city and retreated to Versailles. Now the Central Committee of the National Guard was the sovereign power in Paris.

Although a full overview of the history of the Paris Commune is not within the purview of this book, a few words need to be said about this event. Lasting only seventy-two days, the Paris Commune was a courageous effort by the oppressed to overturn social, economic, and political inequality. In its place, the Commune created new institutions of collective power that broke the existing repressive and bureaucratic state apparatus to create a new state based upon universal suffrage, instant recall of delegates, modest pay for elected officials, and the fusion of legislative and executive functions. It replaced the standing army with the people in arms. The Commune attacked the militarism of French society, putting its faith in the unity of all peoples and internationalism. The Commune fulfilled a number of promises during its short existence: it separated church and state; nationalized church property; instituted free, compulsory, democratic and secular education; made strides toward gender equality; and encouraged the formation of cooperatives in abandoned workshops. Communists, socialists, and anarchists across the world such as Karl Marx and Mikhail Bakunin hailed the Commune as the foundation of a new social system that pointed the way past capitalism.

BLANQUISTS AND THE PARIS COMMUNE

Blanqui was in prison during the Paris Commune, but his supporters were present during the revolution. The Blanquists had members in the important positions in both the National Guard and the Communal Council. They were seemingly well positioned to play a commanding role in the Commune. So what did they do?

Blanqui's "critical support" for the Third Republic's war effort in his journal *La Patrie en Danger* in September and October of 1870 had confused and disoriented the Blanquist party. According to the Blanquist militant Gaston Da Costa,

> We cannot say this often enough: since the besieging of Paris by the
> Prussians, the Blanquist party had sent its men into the battalions of the
> National Guard, and in doing so lost all cohesion.... Blanqui's cry of "the
> fatherland in danger," as meritorious as it was, was also a disintegrating
> factor for the revolutionary forces it disposed of until then.[37]

The Third Republic was unwilling and unable to implement
Blanqui's proposed measures. This led Blanqui to turn against the
Republic and participate in the failed coup of October 31, 1870. After
the coup collapsed, he went into hiding and was only caught the day
before the foundation of the Commune. His capture left the Blanquist party leaderless at the critical hour.

The Blanquists held several leadership positions in the National
Guard, but Hutton states they "did not act as a consolidated interest
group."[38] The Blanquist general Émile Eudes proposed constructing
a revolutionary army led by fellow Blanquist commanders Émile
Duval, Emmanuel Chauvière, Théophile Ferré, and himself. This
plan did not get off the ground and was quashed by the Central Committee of the National Guard.[39]

On the morrow of the revolution, Blanquists in the National
Guard, such as Duval, argued for an immediate offensive against Versailles. Da Costa wrote in retrospect: "Political and social revolution
still lay in the future. And to accomplish it the assembly that had
sold us out had to be constrained by force or dissolve.... It would
not be by striking it with decrees and proclamations that a breach in
the Versailles Assembly would be achieved, but by striking it with
cannonballs."[40]

The chances for a swift military victory appeared promising since
the Commune possessed a potential military force of nearly 200,000
National Guardsmen.[41]

According to the historian Alistair Horne, Thiers's government
at Versailles had few loyal National Guard units under its command:
"The 'reliable' units of the National Guard in Paris, which under the
siege had once numbered between fifty and sixty battalions, could
now be reckoned at little more than twenty; compared with some
three hundred dissident battalions, now liberally equipped with can-
non."[42] Thousands of regular troops were still German POWs, while

those remaining in Versailles lacked discipline and were viewed as susceptible to revolutionary propaganda.

Despite the Paris Commune's military weaknesses and disorganization, its enemy was in an even worse state, and a swift blow could topple them. Instead of going on the attack, the National Guard relinquished their power and called for an election on March 26 to legalize the revolution by creating a commune. On March 30, the Paris Commune abolished conscription and the standing army.

With an offensive now ruled out, the Commune began negotiations with Versailles hoping to avoid bloodshed and secure municipal liberties.[43] Moderates in both the Commune and the National Assembly made several futile, almost comical, efforts to broker a compromise. This was a forlorn hope since Thiers and Versailles recognized at the very onset that this was a civil revolution. The problem was that this energy could not be channeled into an effective fighting force. In two months, the Commune went through five war delegates who could not overcome the inherent disorganization of the National Guard or implement a clear strategy. No leadership was forthcoming from the ruling Communal Council, which remained divided into several competing factions—Jacobins, Blanquists, Internationalists, and Proudhonists. The Blanquists and Jacobins supported tighter security measures and a centralized political leadership to wage war, while the Proudhonist majority (and many Internationalists) opposed any thought of "Jacobin centralism." According to Horne, the Commune's lack of leadership, inconsistent strategy, and factionalism all served to benefit Versailles:

> Thus, from the day it assumed office, the danger was apparent that the Commune might be overloaded, indeed overwhelmed, by the sheer diversity of desires as represented by so polygenous a multitude of personalities, ideologies, and interests. And there was no obvious leader to guide the multitude. Had Blanqui been there, it might have been quite a different story. But Blanqui was securely in the hands of Thiers, while Delescluze, the only other possible leader, was so ailing that he would have preferred nothing better than to have retired from the scene altogether. Thiers, it now seemed, had at least made two excellent initial calculations; one was the seizure of Blanqui, and the other had been to force the Communards to commit themselves before either their plans or their policy had time to crystallize.[44]

Despite the Blanquists' efforts, the Commune never overcame its military weaknesses and broke the siege.

Secondly, the Blanquists' proposed emergency measures to fight Versailles were resisted by the Communal Council—who believed these would violate the principles of the revolution and democracy by instituting a one-man dictatorship and Jacobin terror. As the military situation continued to worsen throughout April, the calls grew louder from many outside Blanquist ranks to create a Committee of Public Safety—harkening back to its 1793 predecessor. It was hoped that the success of the original could be repeated again in 1871. This proposal was in line with Blanquist thinking that saw the Commune as a repetition of the Paris Commune of 1792. In later years, Blanqui himself never wrote anything of consequence on the Paris Commune. The Blanquists neither appreciated nor understood the socialist potential of the Commune. Da Costa denied any socialist potential existed in the Commune:

> The insurrection of March 18 was essentially political, republican, patriotic, and, to qualify it with just one epithet, exclusively Jacobin. . . . It is nevertheless impossible to argue that socialist ideas, if not doctrines, were not spoken of within the assembled Commune, but these affirmations remained verbal, platonic, and in any case foreign to the 200,000 rebels who on March 18, 1871, slid cartridges into their rifles in indignation. If they had truly been socialist revolutionaries, which our good bourgeois like to believe, and not indignant Jacobin and patriotic revolutionaries, they would have acted completely differently. . . . Neither Blanqui, if he would have led us, nor his disciples dreamed of creating this environment in 1871. At that time the Blanquists were the only thing that they could be: Jacobin revolutionaries rising up to defend the threatened republic. The idealist socialists assembled in the minority were nothing but dreamers, without a defined socialist program, and their unfortunate tactics consisted in making the people of Paris and the communes of France believe that they had one.[45]

Eventually, a majority on the Communal Council supported the creation of a Committee of Public Safety,[46] but it was led by incapable men who did not use the unlimited powers theoretically at their disposal. Instead, the Committee of Public Safety added to the organizational confusion of the Commune and was unable to prevent the final debacle.

On top of its own organizational difficulties, the Commune had to contend with a hostile press and real threats of subversion. While many Communards believed repressive organs were unnecessary, the Blanquist Rigault, who headed the police force, thought stern measures were needed to combat the counterrevolution. Rigault was a zealous policeman who went after suspected counterrevolutionaries, such as the clergy, and searched monasteries and churches, believing that they held arms and hidden treasure. These repeated searches turned up nothing substantive. When Rigault banned four hostile papers on April 18—*Le Bien Public, Le Soir, La Cloche,* and *L'Opinion Nationale*—his actions were protested in the Communal Council, and there were calls for his resignation, but he managed to stay on. Rigault possessed a fierce revolutionary drive to do what the situation required, but he was viewed by many as "lazy and conceited, a man who reveled in the perquisites of office without being willing to face the responsibilities.... Rigault continued to pass his afternoons in the cafés of the Left Bank, as had long been his custom, and left the bulk of the work to his subordinates."[47] Rigault's fervor was not shared by the majority of the Commune, and his talents were left without being given direction.

Rigault and the rest of the Blanquists recognized that the fatal weakness of the Commune was its lack of clear and decisive leadership. The Blanquists believed their imprisoned leader could fill that gap and lead the revolution to victory. Blanqui's prestige extended far beyond the Blanquists to other factions in the Commune. Initially, he was elected to the Communal Council (in absentia), and there was a motion in the Commune to make him honorary president (instead, that honor fell to Charles Beslay).[48] Rigault spared no effort to free Blanqui and once declared: "Without Blanqui, nothing could be done. With him, everything."[49] In April, after repeated failures to negotiate with Versailles for Blanqui's release, the Commune offered the Archbishop of Paris its most valuable hostage in exchange for l'Enfermé. Thiers refused and the Communards made a final desperate offer to trade all seventy-four of their hostages in exchange for just Blanqui.

Thiers did not budge. Karl Marx said that from the point of view of Thiers, this was a wise decision: "The Commune again and again had offered to exchange the archbishop, and ever so many priests into the bargain, against the single Blanqui, then in the hands of Thiers. Thiers obstinately refused. He knew that with Blanqui he would give to the Commune a head."[50] In the end, Blanqui remained in jail as his comrades were massacred on the streets of Paris.

Despite the great social advancements of the Commune, it lacked both an effective leadership and a military force needed to defeat the counterrevolution. While the Blanquists occupied a number of key posts in the Paris Commune, they remained ineffective and disorganized without Blanqui. They were unable to influence either the military strategy or provide leadership of the Commune, which never overcame its fatal weaknesses. From May 21 to May 28, in what later became known as Bloody Week, a French army of 170,000 men moved into Paris and crushed the revolution, killing at least 20,000 Communards. Blanquists who played prominent roles in the Commune, such as Rigault and Émile Duval, were killed in the ensuing massacre. Tridon would die shortly after. The Blanquist party was effectively destroyed as an organized force, and its remaining members were either in prison or exile.

X. Eternity by the Stars

While imprisoned at Château du Taureau, Blanqui endured conditions as bad as those of Mont-Saint-Michel. He was locked in a cold cell, forbidden to speak with anyone and allowed no visitors. The guards were under orders to shoot Blanqui down if he made the slightest attempt at escape.

During these dark days, he wrote a seventy-six page booklet, *Eternity by the Stars* (published in 1872) as an extended treatise on astronomy. Nearly all of Blanqui's commentators assert that his work contains no major breakthroughs in science.[1] His basic argument was that the universe is infinite in time and space. He claims that there are only a limited set of elements, and because the combination of these elements was finite, "resorting to repetition becomes necessary."[2] Based on these assumptions, Blanqui speculated on the existence of multiple worlds where every person and event is repeated.

Due to the finite combination of matter, Blanqui says that "mankind does not have the same personnel on all similar globes, and each of the globes have, as it were, its own particular Mankind, each of them comes from the same source, and began at the same point, but branches out into a thousand paths, finally leading into different lives and different histories."[3] Based on those assumptions, Blanqui envisions many alternative realities as opposed to fatalistic conceptions of progress and history. As he said:

> For tomorrow, the events and the people will follow their course. For now on, only the unknown is before us. Like the earth's past, its future

will change direction a million times ... the future shall come to an end only when the globe dies. Until then, every second will bring its new bifurcation, the road taken and the road that could have been taken.[4]

Despite the crushing weight of objective conditions, Blanqui believed that human effort and will can create space for action.

On February 15, 1872, Blanqui's solitary confinement finally came to an end. He was taken to Versailles to stand trial for participating in the insurrection of October 31. In his defense, Blanqui argued:

> I am not here because of 31 October, that is the least of my transgressions. Here I represent the Republic, which finds itself put on trial by supporters of monarchy. The government's prosecutor has indicted, one after the other, the revolutions of 1789, 1830, 1848, and that of 4 September; it is in the name of royalist ideas, it is in the name of old rather than new conceptions of law, as he says, that I will be judged here, and it is on these terms that—under your new Republic—I will be condemned.[5]

Blanqui was sentenced to deportation, but the sentence was commuted to life imprisonment on the grounds of ill health. On September 17, he was sent to his new cell at the former monastery of Clairvaux.

XI. Ni dieu ni Maître

B lanqui's conditions at Clairvaux were dismal. He was kept in a dark room, denied access to newspapers and not allowed to communicate with his fellow prisoners (he was allowed to receive visits from his sisters). Even though the weather was dreadfully cold, Blanqui's cell was unheated. In 1877, his health collapsed and he nearly died.[1]

As Blanqui endured captivity, France saw the rebirth of political life. In 1877, republicans won a sweeping majority of seats in the Chamber of Deputies. Two years later, they gained control of the Senate, ending the chances for a monarchist restoration. The stabilization of the Third Republic heartened workers and opened the door to independent political action on their part.

One of the first to take advantage of the mood for leftist politics was a young journalist named Jules Guesde (1845–1922). Guesde, a former republican and anarchist, had been in exile for writing newspaper articles defending the Paris Commune. Returning to France in 1876, he was a now a fiery convert to Marxism and founded *Égalité*. Guesde and *Égalité* became leading voices supporting amnesty for the exiled Communards. The demand for amnesty had wide support from all sectors of the labor movement: left-leaning republicans, socialists, and anarchists. The amnesty campaign centered on Blanqui, the eternal revolutionary and symbol of republican unity.

In 1879, the amnesty campaign nominated Blanqui for a seat in the first constituency of Bordeaux. A mass movement developed as supporters, petitions, and articles backed his election campaign. Garibaldi, the hero of Italian unification, endorsed Blanqui's candidacy. Letters of encouragement from all over France were sent to Blanqui.[2] Even Georges Clemenceau, former Blanquist, spoke up in the Chamber of Deputies in defense of his old mentor: "One might reject Blanqui's views, but no one could either dispute his staunch republicanism, or deny him the dignity he had maintained under the most trying conditions, or impugn his character which was unassailable."[3] On April 29, 1879, Blanqui was elected. There was joyous celebration.

Victory turned to rage when the Chamber of Deputies annulled the election results. This action gave credence to those who argued that the ballot was a useless way of changing things. When the amnesty campaign resumed, the Third Republic could see which way the wind was blowing. They yielded to popular pressure and released Blanqui from prison. On June 10, 1879, after nine years in hellish conditions, Blanqui was freed.

Blanqui was now seventy-four years old. He had no plans to retire. The amnesty campaign had shown him that a new generation of revolutionaries and workers were still receptive to his message. So the grand old man got back to work.

One ex-comrade, Paul Lafargue, now a committed Marxist, reached out to him. Lafargue still maintained a healthy respect for Blanqui and wanted him to become part of a new socialist party that he was organizing with Guesde. Lafargue's letter to Blanqui said:

> You are coming out on top . . . when we have the greatest need of a man like [you] to set up the proletarian party and send it forth for the conquest of power . . . [the Commune gave the proletariat] a sense of its historical mission and the revolutionary politics behind it, who have been asking only to be organized in order to be the vanguard of the movement for all humanity.[4]

Lafargue then made his appeal to Blanqui: "You are reemerging to be our standard-bearer."[5] Lafargue invited Blanqui to come to London to discuss the matter with him personally. He also hinted that Marx would be interested in meeting him.[6] There is no evidence that Blanqui answered the invitation. In any case, he did not go to London.

Blanqui had other work to do. He ran again for election in Bordeaux, but his rallies were harassed by the police, and the press slandered him. When the election results came in August, he lost by just 156 votes.

For the next year and a half, Blanqui went on a speaking tour across France, addressing rallies and banquets. He attracted huge crowds; many came not so much for what he said, but to see a living legend. At one rally, he spoke alongside the anarchist Communard Louise Michel. Blanqui went to Italy for a celebration of Garibaldi. He wrote a short pamphlet, *L'armée esclave et opprimée*, arguing for replacing the standing army with a popular militia. He attacked clerical power, supported women's emancipation, and passionately believed that the republic needed to become truly democratic and social.[7] He feared that the republic was still threatened by monarchists and counterrevolutionaries and that the new republican and socialist leaders were not up to the challenge of defending it. In 1880, he wrote to a friend: "Whenever I revolted I was impelled by the most imperious and sacred duty. I greatly fear that the baseness of opportunism imposes this duty on us again."[8] Most of his efforts were devoted to working for amnesty of the Communards, which was finally granted in July 1880.

The amnesty of the Communards allowed his exiled comrades to finally come home. With returned members of the Blanquist party, he founded a newspaper, *Ni Dieu ni Maître*. The paper grounded itself in the French revolutionary tradition (using the republican calendar), but also discussed labor struggles, attacked the Church, and demanded free secular education. Blanqui locked horns with one of the editors, Édouard Vaillant, who wrote from a Marxist-influenced perspective.[9]

Blanqui kept up a frenzied pace, and in December 1880, he spoke at four meetings in Paris. At a meeting on December 27, when the crowd cheered for the tricolor, Blanqui said his loyalty belonged only to the red flag. Afterward, he returned home to the apartment that he shared with Ernest Granger, a young Blanquist. While speaking together, Blanqui suddenly got up and then collapsed onto the floor. He had suffered a stroke of apoplexy and was in a coma. On January 1, 1881, he passed away.

His funeral on January 5 attracted a huge crowd of 200,000 people, many of them from abroad. Whether they were anarchists, Marxists, Proudhonists, or republicans, all of them wished to pay their last respects. The crowd marched to Père Lachaise Cemetery, where the last Communards had been executed and Blanqui was laid to rest. The Blanquists Émile Eudes and Èdouard Vaillant gave their eulogies, as did Louise Michel. The Russian revolutionary Peter Tkachev delivered a final address: "He is the uncontested chief who has filled us with revolutionary faith, the resolution to struggle, the scorn of suffering."[10]

Blanqui had fallen.

Conclusion:
The Unconquered

Blanqui's life was devoted to revolutionary struggle and the overthrow of capitalism. He was not willing to compromise on the goal. There was no divorce in him between theory and practice. He was formed to act—to act earnestly and without romantic illusions about what it would take to win. He asked the right questions, even if he provided the wrong answers, about how to make a revolution. Blanqui believed that a disciplined conspiracy could enable the working class to challenge the powerful and open new roads leading to the reign of equality. As he said, "But the day after a revolution, a coup de théâtre occurs. It is not that a sudden transformation takes place all at once. Men and things remain the same as before. It is just that hope and fear have changed sides. The chains fall, the nation is free, and an immense horizon opens up before it."[1] It was not so. Blanqui's plans allowed no room for the workers in their own liberation, and they proved more than capable of organizing without the aid of an elite conspiracy.

Still, Blanqui's courage, talents as an organizer, and his willingness to endure everything are not subject to question. He was the heir of the Jacobin revolutionary tradition and the forerunner of the new socialist one. To the bourgeoisie, he was the embodiment of the specter of communism. To the working class, he was their hero and hope. Whatever else we can say about Blanqui, he fought against the odds, and, in the end, his revolutionary spirit was never conquered.

141

EPILOGUE:
THE FATE OF BLANQUISM

Following Blanqui's death in 1881, his followers, led by Édouard Vaillant, Émile Eudes, and Ernest Granger, organized the Central Revolutionary Committee (CRC) to continue the revolutionary struggle. However, times had changed, and the age of conspiracy was giving way to mass politics. The Blanquists struggled to find their place in the Third Republic. They became guardians of the French revolutionary tradition, celebrating anniversaries of the past and treating people like Blanqui as martyrs and saints. They hoped that by keeping the memories of struggle alive that they could reignite the Jacobin and revolutionary spirit among the people and spur them into action. The Blanquist perspective was fundamentally backward looking. There was no critical analysis of the Commune or Blanqui, just the commemoration of myths and legends. By contrast, the other socialist parties and labor organizations were more attuned than the Blanquists to the possibilities of mass politics.

Some Blanquists such as Édouard Vaillant, who had been in contact with Marxists while in exile, understood that new political methods were called for: running candidates in elections, printing newspapers, and utilizing other modes of propaganda. To the traditionalists, this was a sign that Vaillant was moving away from the goal of a Blanquist-led insurrection.

As the 1880s wore on, the Blanquists found themselves drawn, against their own expectations, into electoral politics. Following the

143

Jacobin tradition, they championed the interests of the "people" and looked to ally with others who shared a populist vision. In 1887, the Blanquists were drawn to the anti-Semitic, nationalist, and populist movement surrounding General Georges Boulanger. The Blanquists supported the Boulangist movement, believing the general would stage a coup to overthrow the Third Republic, which they viewed as decadent and corrupt.

Vaillant was not willing to go this far, and the Blanquist party split in 1888. A minority of Blanquists agreed with Vaillant, remaining in the CRC. The majority of Blanquists stayed loyal to Boulanger and formed the Socialist Revolutionary Central Committee (CCSR). When the Boulangist movement collapsed in scandal the following year, the CCSR was discredited as a revolutionary organization. In the ensuing decade, they moved far away from Blanquism and social-ism, embracing a virulent nationalism and anti-Semitism before fad-ing into oblivion.

The CRC formally embraced Marxism in 1892. Ten years later, they merged with the Marxist-led Parti Ouvrier Français of Jules Guesde to form the Parti socialiste de France. In 1905, under pres-sure from the Second International, the Parti socialiste de France fused with other socialist groups to form the Section Française de l'Internationale Ouvrière (SFIO) or the French Section of the Wor-kers' International. Now French Socialists were united into a single party with a Marxist program led by Jules Guesde, Jean Jaurès, Édouard Vaillant, and Paul Lafargue. Vaillant remained in the SFIO as a respected leader until his death in 1915, but Blanquism as a sep-arate political trend passed into history.

The epilogue draws on the following texts: Doug Enaa Greene, "The Rise of Marxism in France," *LINKS International Journal of Socialist Renewal*. http://links.org.au/node/4684; Hal Draper, *Karl Marx's Theory of Revolution*, vol. IV: *Critique of Other Socialisms* (New York: Monthly Review Press, 1990): 204–37; William D. Irvine, *The Boulanger Affair Reconsidered: Royalism, Boulangism, and the Origins of the Radical Right in France* (New York: Oxford University Press, 1989); Patrick Hutton, "Popular Boulangism and the Advent of Mass Politics in France, 1886–90," *Journal of Contemporary History* 11.1 (Jan., 1976): 85–106; Paul Mazgaj, "The Origins of the French Radical Right: A Historiographical Essay," *French Historical Studies* 15.2 (Autumn, 1987): 287–315; Bruce Fulton, "The Boulanger Affair Revisited: The Preservation of the Third Republic, 1889," *French Historical Studies* 17.2 (Autumn, 1991): 310–29; George L. Mosse, "The French Right and the Working Classes: Les Jaunes," *Journal of Contemporary History* 7.3 (July-Oct., 1972): 185–208; Hutton 1981, 119–73; Patrick Hutton, "The Role of the Blanquist Party in Left-Wing Politics in France, 1879–90," *Journal of Modern History* 46.2 (Jun., 1974): 277–95; Jolyon Michael Howorth, "The Myth of Blanquism under the Third Republic (1871–1900)," *Journal of Modern History* 48. 3 (Sept., 1976): 37–68; Stuart 1992; Bernstein 1971, 355–57.

Appendix: Marxist Assessments of Blanqui

Marx and Engels

By the late 1840s, Marx and Engels had developed a new communist theory of history and society that claimed the working class was the only revolutionary class under capitalism that was diametrically opposed to Blanquism. Their theory of proletarian revolution is based on the following premises: capitalism draws the working class together and organizes them. The workers' conditions of life compels them to struggle and organize. The interests of the working class as a whole, regardless of whether they are consciously revolutionary, are diametrically opposed to the interests of capital, which leads them to struggle. The workers' organized struggle leads them to challenge both bourgeois ideas and institutions. Members of the working class have decisive social weight in capitalism, due to their strategic position in the economy as the creators of wealth. When the working class goes into action, it shakes all of society because the existence of the bourgeoisie depends on it. In the last instance, it is in the interests of the working class and its struggles to transform and reconstruct society on a communist basis.[1] Whereas Blanquists believed that workers could only be liberated by an elite conspiracy, Marx and Engels argued the opposite: "The emancipation of the working classes must be conquered by the working classes themselves."[2]

Despite their theoretical disagreements with Blanquism, Marx and Engels held Blanqui, the man, in high esteem as a devoted, principled, and honest revolutionary. In one 1861 letter, Marx said of Blanqui: "Rest assured that there is no one more interested than myself in the lot of a man whom I have always regarded as the brains and inspiration of the proletarian party in France."[3] Whenever Blanqui was attacked, whether by Barbès' slanders or the political persecution of Napoleon III, Marx and Engels rose to defend him.

Blanqui the individual may have been admirable, but Marx and Engels's entire theoretical and political practice remained firmly anti-Blanquist. When Marx and Engels did occasionally ally with Blanquists, it was always in the interest of developing a broad-based international political movement. They never once surrendered any principles to ally with Blanquism, nor did they ever organize conspiracies instead of independent working-class parties.

When Marx and Engels first became acquainted with the League of the Just in the 1840s, the organization was under the influence of the Blanquist ideas of Wilhelm Weitling, and they refused to join it. In 1847, when they finally did join the League (soon renamed the Communist League), it was not because they embraced Blanquism. Far from it: Marx and Engels joined the League because it rejected the elitist trappings of secret societies and organized itself on a democratic basis. As Engels said in his *History of the Communist League*:

> Suffice it to say that in the spring of 1847 Moll visited Marx in Brussels nd immediately afterwards myself in Paris, and invited us repeatedly, in the name of his comrades, to join the League. He reported that they were as much convinced of the general correctness of our views as of the need to free the League from the old conspiratorial traditions and forms. Should we join, we would be given an opportunity of expounding our critical communism before a congress of the League in a manifesto, which would then be published as the manifesto of the League; we would likewise be able to contribute our quota towards the replacement of the obsolete League organization by one in keeping with the new times and aims.[4]

The new role of the Communist League was to serve as a guide for the workers on the path of liberation, not to act in their place.

In light of the defeats of 1848, Marx and Engels attempted to convince the League that a new revolutionary movement would result from changes in the economic situation, which would be based upon a broad class alliance led by the workers who would lead a permanent revolution culminating in communism.[5] Other factions in the League, led by August Willich and Karl Schnapper, believed that a revolution could be imposed by a minority through an act of will, regardless of the economic situation. Marx and Engels ridiculed this Blanquist conception at a meeting of the League in September 1850:

> The revolution is seen not as the product of realities of the situation but as the result of an effort of will. Whereas we say to the workers: You have 15, 20, 50 years of civil war to go through in order to alter the situation and to train yourselves for the exercise of power, it is said: We must take power at once, or else we may as well take to our beds.[6]

The breach between the two camps could not be bridged, and a few months later, the League split. Shortly afterward, Marx resigned and the League itself dissolved.[7]

Earlier in 1850, when Marx and Engels still hoped for a new revolutionary wave, they were willing to ally with Blanquist groups in London exile. This alliance was based on practical considerations: political conditions in Europe precluded open and mass working-class organizations, leaving room for only secret societies. If Marx and Engels wanted to be involved in revolutionary politics on the continent, they had no option except working with groups like the Blanquists.[8] To that end, in April 1850, Marx and Engels joined with the Blanquists to form a united front and international organization known as the Société Universelle des Communistes Révolutionnaires (SCUR), which released a joint manifesto with one of the first recorded mentions of the phrase "dictatorship of the proletariat."[9] Hal Draper argues that the SCUR statutes were "no doubt the outcome of some preliminary discussion, but may not have been regarded as final—only as a basis for further negotiation."[10] The evidence shows that Marx and Engels did not accept the Blanquist view of an elite dictatorship over the proletariat; for them the dictatorship of the proletariat meant the rule of the workers as a class.[11] Nor did Blanqui ever use that term. According to Alan Spitzer, "Blanqui had often been credited with coining the phrase 'the dictatorship of the proletariat' but no one has ever been able to document his use of it upon any occasion."[12]

While the SCUR was formed with the highest aspirations, it remained stillborn. By October, the project was abandoned by Marx and Engels once they realized that there was no prospect of an immediate revolution in Europe. Instead, they changed tactics to focus on propaganda and education.[13] There is no further mention of SCUR in the statutes of the Communist League or in the correspondence of Marx, Engels, or the writings of Blanqui.

While Marx was building the abortive united front with the Blanquists, he reviewed two books by former Parisian police spies. In those reviews, Marx provided his most sustained and penetrating critique of Blanquism. According to Marx, the view of the police and the Blanquist conspirators were simply mirror images of each other. Both saw revolution as the result of actions by small determined groups, not broad social forces.

Marx criticized the Blanquists for being cut off from the majority of the working class and artificially fomenting revolutions:

> It is precisely their business to anticipate the process of revolutionary development, to bring it artificially to crisis-point, to launch a revolution on the spur of the moment, without the conditions for a revolution. For them the only condition for revolution is the adequate preparation of their conspiracy. They are the alchemists of the revolution and are characterized by exactly the same chaotic thinking and blinkered obsessions as the alchemists of old. They leap at inventions which are supposed to work revolutionary miracles: incendiary bombs, destructive devices of magic effect, revolts which are expected to be all the more miraculous and astonishing in effect as their basis is less rational. Occupied with such scheming, they have no other purpose than the most immediate one of overthrowing the existing government and have the profoundest contempt for the more theoretical enlightenment of the proletariat about their class interests.[14]

From 1851 until the Paris Commune, there are only scattered mentions of Blanqui and Blanquism in Marx and Engels's work.

Since the Blanquists played a prominent role in the Commune, they naturally took note of it. Engels's conclusions of Blanquist activities was not very flattering. He observed that they "did the opposite of what the doctrines of their school proscribed."[15]

Despite this, the Blanquists found themselves supporting Marx, Engels, and the First International. The reason is simple: Marx was the public leader of the First International who wrote *The Civil War in France* in May 1871, an eloquent and powerful defense of the Commune, while there was still fighting in the streets of Paris. This was a brave act for Marx to undertake while the bourgeois press of Europe and America accused the Paris Commune of horrific atrocities and of threatening to destroy western civilization.

Secondly, the International led efforts to organize relief for Communard refugees in London. Among these exiles were Blanquists. The Blanquists reassembled in London, forming their own mutual aid society to assist refugees and establish a new political grouping— The Revolutionary Commune. Engels says that those in the Revolutionary Commune were "called Blanquists not because they are a group founded by Blanqui—of the 33 signatories to the programme only a few may ever have spoken to Blanqui—but because they want to act in his spirit and in accordance with his tradition."[16]

A number of prominent Communards who had not been members of the old Blanquist party joined the Revolutionary Commune, notably Édouard Vaillant, Frédéric Cournet, and Gabriel Ranvier. Vaillant was a rising star in the Blanquist movement. He was a talented journalist and open to a variety of new ideas, such as Marxism, in a way that made the old guard of Blanquists very uncomfortable.

It was only natural that the Blanquists (such as Vaillant) looked upon the International and Marx, the only public defender of the Commune, in a positive light. While the Blanquists were hostile to the Proudhonist-dominated French section of the International in the 1860s, Marx's belief in political action impressed them. The rapprochement between the two groups gained impetus in April 1872, after the International expelled Henri Tolain, a Proudhonist and a former leader of the French section, because he supported Versailles against the Commune.[17] Marx and Engels were optimistic that the

Blanquists could now be won over to their views. The close cooperation between the two groups led the International to co-opt a number
of the Blanquists such as Édouard Vaillant, Gabriel Ranvier, Anton-
ie Arnaud, Frédéric Cournet, and Jules Johannard.[18] In September
1871, the Blanquists attended a banquet to celebrate the founding
of the International, where Marx gave a speech upholding the Paris
Commune as the dictatorship of the proletariat.[19]

Still, Marx and Engels disagreed with the Blanquists over how
to assess the meaning of the Commune. Marx hailed the Commune
as the forerunner of future proletarian revolutions. The Blanquists
viewed the Commune as "the recreation of the revolutionary community of 1793" and "conceived of themselves as a vanguard of professional revolutionaries dating from the Hébertists."[20] Marx stressed
the international significance of the Commune for the working class,
but the Blanquists "while sympathetic to oppressed peoples everywhere, envisioned their revolution as an autonomous uprising, turning on a nativist conception of community."[21] These two balance
sheets of the Paris Commune could not be reconciled.

Marx wanted the Blanquists' support against Mikhail Bakunin
and his efforts to wreck the International. By late 1872, the factional
fighting in the International was reaching its pitch. During the Hague
Congress, Vaillant introduced an anti-anarchist resolution in favor
of independent political action by the working class. He attacked the
Bakuninists and Proudhonists for their abstentionism and their opposition to "the conquest of state power."[22] After the Marxists and the
Blanquists voted to expel the Bakuninists, the united front between the
two forces quickly evaporated. Marx opposed the Blanquists' political
strategy that called for immediate revolutionary action in France. He
believed that a long non-revolutionary period awaited Europe. In an
effort to outmaneuver the Blanquists and prevent them from control of
the International, Marx proposed moving the organization's headquar-
ters to New York. After Marx's proposal passed, the Blanquists left the
International (that itself soon passed into oblivion).

After the Blanquists left the International, they condemned
Marx's political maneuvering and "denounced [the International]
for its abstract conception of internationalism and reaffirmed [their]

commitment to the French Revolutionary tradition."[23] The Blanquists, all forty-four of them, retreated back into their own group, Revolutionary Commune, where they attempted to chart a new path under Vaillant's leadership.

When the Blanquists released a public declaration of principles, *Aux Communeux*, in 1874, Engels criticized the document as nothing more than a restatement of classical Blanquist positions. Engels offered a succinct criticism of Blanquism and its worldview that is worth quoting at length:

> Blanqui is essentially a political revolutionary, a socialist only in sentiment, because of his sympathy for the sufferings of the people, but he has neither socialist theory nor definite practical proposals for social reforms. In his political activities he was essentially a "man of action," believing that, if a small well-organized minority should attempt to effect a revolutionary uprising at the right moment, it might, after scoring a few initial successes, carry the mass of the people and thus accomplish a victorious revolution.... Since Blanqui regards every revolution as a coup de main by a small revolutionary minority, it automatically follows that its victory must inevitably be succeeded by the establishment of a dictatorship—not, it should be well noted, of the entire revolutionary class, the proletariat, but of the small number of those who accomplished the coup and who themselves are, at first, organized under the dictatorship of one or several individuals.
>
> Obviously, Blanqui is a revolutionary of the old generation.[24]

Despite his criticism, Engels adds, "Some definite progress can be noted in this programme. It is the first manifesto in which French workers rally to the cause of present-day German communism."[25] The program showed that some of them, such as Vaillant, were adopting Marxist terminology, but that did not change the underlying Blanquist ideas.

Marx and Engels respected Blanqui and were willing to form temporary blocs with the Blanquists, but their politics were not based on elite conspiracies but upon the self-emancipation of the working class.

REVISIONISM

By the turn of the twentieth century, Blanqui and Blanquism had been largely forgotten in the socialist movement, now largely organized in the Second International. As Walter Benjamin observed:

> In the course of three decades [social democracy] succeeded in almost completely erasing the name of Blanqui, whose distant thunder had made the preceding century tremble. It contented itself with assigning the working-class the role of the savior of future generations. It thereby severed the sinews of its greatest power. Through this schooling the class forgot its hate as much as its spirit of sacrifice. For both nourish themselves on the picture of enslaved forebears, not on the ideal of the emancipated heirs.[26]

The Second International claimed to be committed to socialism, but inside, many parties were members known as revisionists, who advocated the whole-scale abandonment of revolutionary Marxism. In the German Social Democratic Party (SPD), the revisionist case was put forth by Eduard Bernstein, who wrote a series of articles between 1896 and 1898 that argued that socialists should focus on winning elected offices and gradual reforms. Bernstein claimed that socialism could be established without recourse to revolution.[27]

In updating Marxism, Bernstein claimed that it had to be purged of "Blanquism," which had infected the youthful works of Marx and Engels. According to Bernstein, the source of Marx and Engels's "Blanquism" was the Hegelian dialectic, which was a "theory of the immeasurable creative power of revolutionary political force and its manifestation, revolutionary expropriation" and could be found in *The Communist Manifesto*.[28] Bernstein concluded that "the great things Marx and Engels achieved were achieved not because of Hegelian dialectic but in spite of it. When, on the other hand, they heedlessly passed over the greatest errors of Blanquism, it is primarily the Hegelian element in their theory that is to blame."[29]

Rosa Luxemburg argued that Bernstein could only accuse Marx and Engels of "Blanquism" by extending the definition of the word so much that it didn't mean a coup d'etat, but anything revolutionary:

Bernstein, thundering against the conquest of political power as a theory of Blanquist violence, has the misfortune of labeling as a Blanquist error that which has always been the pivot and the motive force of human history. From the first appearance of class societies having the class struggle as the essential content of their history, the conquest of political power has been the aim of all rising classes.[30]

Bernstein's revisionist crusade against the residues of "Blanquism" in Marxism was really just masked condemnation for any and all advocacy of socialist revolution.

BOLSHEVISM

When the Russian Revolution occurred in 1917, it was not only the revisionists but also orthodox Marxists, such as the respected theorist Karl Kautsky, who condemned it as inspired by "pre-Marxist ways of thought . . . represented by Blanqui, Weitling or Bakunin."[31] Even those sympathetic to both Blanquism and Bolshevism, such as Maurice Dommanget, linked the two: "The liaison between Babouvism and Bolshevism by way of revolutionary Marxism is realized, so to speak, through Blanquism."[32]

Among both radicals and anti-communists, the belief that the October Revolution was a Leninist minority coup or an example of Blanquism has practically been an article of faith.[33] The mountain of evidence belies any claim that Bolshevism was in any way, shape, or form Blanquist. Lenin flatly denied it: "To become a power the class-conscious workers must win the majority to their side. . . . We are not Blanquists, we do not stand for the seizure of power by a minority."[34] The practice of Bolshevism throughout 1917 was one of "patient explanation," in which the party conducted open agitation among the workers, peasants, and soldiers. When the Bolsheviks took power, it was not done on behalf of a single party but based upon the soviets—organs of working-class democracy—with whom they had won a majority.

However, there is still a grain of truth that the October Revolution was Blanquist. Revolutionaries, whether Marx, Engels, Lenin, or

Trotsky, needed to ask the questions: What is a revolutionary situation? What are the strategies and tactics that lead to the conquest of power? How can insurrection be treated as an art? Blanqui had spent decades of his life treating insurrection as an art. Lenin and Trotsky took seriously questions of insurrection, military strategy, and the nature of power. Naturally, Blanqui was not condemned by them for doing the same. Trotsky recognized his positive contribution in that regard:

> Insurrection is an art, and like all arts it has its laws. The rules of Blanqui were the demands of a military revolutionary realism. . . . Conspiracy does not take the place of insurrection. An active minority of the proletariat, no matter how well organized, cannot seize the power regardless of the general conditions of the country. In this point history has condemned Blanquism. But only in this. His affirmative theorem retains all its force. In order to conquer the power, the proletariat needs more than a spontaneous insurrection. It needs a suitable organization, it needs a plan: it needs a conspiracy. Such is the Leninist view of this question.[35]

In contrast to Blanquism, the Bolsheviks did not base their revolution on a conspiracy but on a rising movement led by the working class. Lenin articulated the fundamental differences between the Blanquist and Marxist approaches to insurrection as follows:

> Marxists are accused of Blanquism for treating insurrection as an art! Can there be a more flagrant perversion of the truth, when not a single Marxist will deny that it was Marx who expressed himself on this score in the most definite, precise and categorical manner, referring to insurrection specifically as an art, saying that it must be treated as an art, that you must win the first success and then proceed from success to success, never ceasing the offensive against the enemy, taking advantage of his confusion, etc., etc.? To be successful, insurrection must rely not upon conspiracy and not upon a party, but upon the advanced class. That is the first point. Insurrection must rely upon a revolutionary upsurge of the people. That is the second point. Insurrection must rely upon that turning-point in the history of the growing revolution when the activity of the advanced ranks of the people is at its height, and when the vacillations in the ranks of the enemy and in the ranks of the weak, half-hearted and irresolute friends of the revolution are strongest. That is the third point. And these three conditions for raising the question of insurrection distinguish Marxism from Blanquism.[36]

Both Lenin and Trotsky gave Blanqui his due, but their approaches to insurrection were polar opposites to his. Bolshevism can only be called "Blanquist" in the sense that it earnestly thought about how the working class could actually take and exercise power.

This Bolshevik legacy was inherited by the early Soviet Union, which did not fear the stigma of Blanquism. The Communist International's 1928 book *Armed Insurrection* said Bernstein and the Second International called communists Blanquists in order to slander them: "Bernstein, in his time, accused Marx of Blanquism. Today it is the entire Second International which accuses the Communist International of Blanquism, and equates Blanquism with communism. In slandering the communists in this way, the social democrats represent Blanqui, the committed revolutionary of the past, as a petty-bourgeois fanatic."[37]

Later, as the Soviet Union bureaucratized and became conservative, any talk of insurrection or revolution was condemned as unrealistic, an embarrassment, or ultra-leftist. An important Soviet textbook, *Scientific Communism,* described Blanqui as a "utopian communist" in order to casually dismiss him.[38] The pro-Soviet Communist Parties, once bastions of world revolution, by the 1930s saw every manifestation of militancy as "Blanquist."

There were a few voices within the Moscow-aligned communist parties who refused to dismiss Blanqui, such as the French communist André Marty. Marty was a leader of the Black Fleet Mutiny of 1919 and head of the International Brigades in Spain. He believed that in 1944, the French Communist Party (PCF) should have transformed the liberation of France from the Nazi occupation into a bid for power. Marty's 1951 speech at the Société des Amis de Blanqui was more than simply upholding the legacy of Blanqui; it was arguably a veiled criticism of the PCF's abandonment of its revolutionary mission. According to Marty: "But what the bourgeois socialists never forgave Blanqui for was his denunciation of their class collaboration and class betrayal." When Marty uttered those words, the PCF had just been forced out of a French government where they had collaborated with bourgeois ministers and broken strikes. Marty praised

Blanqui for his revolutionary commitment to the workers. There was perhaps a hint of irony when Marty celebrated Blanqui for having "never retreated," and then said that "Blanqui lacked a great workers' party of a new type—the French Communist Party."[39] The following year, Marty was expelled from the PCF and the party continued on its non-revolutionary path.

Marxists such as Lenin, Luxemburg, and Trotsky agreed with Marx's criticism of Blanqui, but they recognized that when their opponents condemned them as "Blanquists," it was not because they actually were. As Trotsky said: "The revisionists label the revolutionary content of Marxism with the word Blanquism, the more easily to enable them to fight against Marxism."[40] When revolutionaries were rebuked for Blanquism, it was not because they shared Blanqui's vices, but because they upheld his virtues—his willingness to struggle against the odds, treating insurrection as an art, and his uncompromising revolutionary communism.

BIBLIOGRAPHY

WORKS BY BLANQUI

Abidor, Mitchell, ed. *Communards: The Story of The Paris Commune of 1871 as Told by Those Who Fought for It*. Pacifica CA: Marxists Internet Archive, 2010.

———, ed. *The Great Anger: Ultra-Revolutionary Writings from the Atheist Priest to the Bonnot Gang*. Pacifica CA: Marxists Internet Archive, 2009.

Blanqui, Louis-Auguste. *Critique Sociale, Volume 1 Capital et travail*. Paris: Félix Alcan, 1885a.

———. *Critique Sociale Volume 2: Fragments et notes*. Paris: Félix Alcan, 1885.

———. *Eternity by the Stars*. New York: Contra Mundum Press, 2013.

———. *Maintenant, il faut des armes*, ed. Dominique Le Nuz. Paris: La fabrique éditions, 2006.

———. *Textes choisis*, ed. V.P. Volguine. Paris: Éditions Sociales, 1956.

The Blanqui Archive. https://blanqui.kingston.ac.uk/.

Louis-Auguste Blanqui Archive. http://www.marxistsfr.org/reference/archive/blanqui/.

SECONDARY SOURCES

Abendroth, Wolfgang. *A Short History of the European Working Class*. New York: Monthly Review Press, 1972.

Allison, John M. S. "Paris after the July Days." *The Sewanee Review* 31.1 (Jan., 1923): 60–72.

Aminzade, Ronald. "Reinterpreting Capitalist Industrialization: A Study of Nineteenth Century France." *Social History* 9.3 (1984): 329–50.

Beaud, Michel. *A History of Capitalism 1500–1980*. New York: Monthly Review Press, 1983.

Benjamin, Walter. *The Arcades Project.* Cambridge: Harvard University Press, 1999.

———. *Illuminations.* New York: Schocken Books, 1968.

———. *Walter Benjamin: Selected Writings: Volume 4, 1938–1940.* Edited by Howard Eiland and Michael W. Jennings. Cambridge: Harvard University Press, 2003.

Bensaïd, Daniel, and Michael Löwy. "Auguste Blanqui, Heretical Communist." *Radical Philosophy* 185 (May/June 2014): 26–35.

Bernstein, Eduard. *The Preconditions of Socialism.* New York: University of Cambridge, 1993.

Bernstein, Samuel. *The Beginnings of Marxian Socialism in France.* New York: Russell & Russell, 1965.

———. "Buonarroti's Classic History of Babouvism." *Science & Society* 21.4 (Fall, 1957): 346–52.

———. *Essays in Political and Intellectual History.* New York: Paine-Whitman Publishers, 1955a.

———. "The First International on the Eve of the Paris Commune." *Science & Society* 5.1 (Fall 1941): 29–56.

———. "Jules Guesde, Pioneer of Marxism in France." *Science & Society* 4.1 (Winter 1940b): 24–42.

———. *Louis-Auguste Blanqui and the Art of Insurrection.* London: Lawrence & Wishart, 1971.

———. "Marx in Paris, 1848: A Neglected Chapter." *Science & Society* 3.3 (Summer 1939): 323–55.

———, et al. "Marx and Engels in Paris, 1848: Supplementary Documents." *Science & Society* 5.1 (Spring, 1940a): 211–17.

———. "The Paris Commune." *Science & Society,* 5, No. 2 (Spring 1941): 117–47.

———. "Saint Simon's Philosophy of History." *Science & Society* 12, 1(Winter, 1948): 82–6.

———. "Some Recent Historical Literature: From the Enlightenment to the Commune." *Science and Society* 22.4 (Fall 1958): 330–55.

———. "Trends in French Socialism, 1789–1871." *Science and Society* 11.1 (Winter 1947): 1–10.

———. "Two Historical Methods." *Science and Society* 19.4 (Fall 1955b): 320–33.

Bezucha, Robert J. *The Lyon Uprising of 1834: Social and Political Conflict in the Early July Monarchy.* Cambridge: Harvard University Press, 1974.

Billington, James H. *Fire in the Minds of Men: Origins of the Revolutionary Faith.* New York: Basic Books, Inc., Publishers, 1980.

Birchall, Ian. "The Enigma of Kersausie: Engels in June 1848 (2002)." *Marx-*

ists Internet Archive. http://www.marxists.org/history/etol/writers/birchall/2002/xx/kersausie.htm.

———. *The Spectre of Babeuf.* Chicago: Haymarket, 2016.

———. "Why Did Walter Benjamin Misrepresent Blanqui?" *Grim and Dim.* http://grimanddim.org/historical-writings/2016-why-did-walter-benjamin-misrepresent-Blanqui/.

Buonarroti, Philippe. *History of Babeuf's Conspiracy for Equality.* London: H. Hetherinton, 1836.

Da Costa, Charles. *Les Blanquistes.* Paris: Librairie des Sciences Politiques et Sociales, 1912.

Decaux, Alain. *Blanqui, L'Insurgé: La Passion de la révolution.* Paris: Librairie académique Perrin, 1976.

Derfler, Leslie. *Paul Lafargue and the Founding of French Marxism, 1842–1882.* Cambridge MA: Harvard University Press, 1991.

Deutscher, Isaac. *Heretics and Renegades.* New York: Bobbs-Merrill Company, Inc., 1957.

———. *Stalin.* New York: Penguin Books, 1977.

Dommanget, Maurice. *Blanqui à Belle-Île.* Paris: Librairie du Travail, 1935.

———. "La vie de Blanqui sous le Second Empire: De la Sortie de Belle-Île a la Sortie de Sainte-Pélagie (1er Decembre 1857–12 Mars 1864)." *Le Mouvement social,* No. 35 (Apr. - Jun., 1961), 30–41.

———. *Blanqui.* Paris: Études et documentation internationales, 1970.

Draper, Hal. *Karl Marx's Theory of Revolution Volume 1: State and Bureaucracy.* New York: Monthly Review Press, 1977.

———. *Karl Marx's Theory of Revolution Volume 2: The Politics of Social Classes.* New York: Monthly Review Press, 1978.

———. *Karl Marx's Theory of Revolution Volume 3: The "Dictatorship of the Proletariat."* New York: Monthly Review Press: 1986.

———. *Karl Marx's Theory of Revolution, Volume 4: Critique of Other Socialisms.* New York: Monthly Review Press, 1990.

Dunham, Arthur L. "Industrial Life and Labor in France 1815–1848." *Journal of Economic History* 3.3 (November 1943), 117–51.

Edwards, Stewart. ed. *The Communards of Paris, 1871.* Ithaca: Cornell University Press, 1973.

———. *The Paris Commune 1871.* New York: Quadrangle Books, 1971.

Eisenstein, Elizabeth. *The First Professional Revolutionist: Filippo Buonarroti (1761–1837).* Cambridge: Harvard University Press, 1959.

Eley, Geoff. *Forging Democracy: The History of the Left in Europe, 1850–2000.* New York: Oxford University Press, 2002.

Elliott-Bateman, Michael, John Ellis, and Tom Bowden, ed. *Revolt to Revolution: Studies in the 19th and 20th Century European Experience,* Fourth Dimension of Warfare: Vol. 2. Manchester: Manchester University Press, 1974.

Fedoseyev, P. N. ed. *Scientific Communism.* Moscow: Progress Publishers, 1983.

Fishman, William J. *The Insurrectionists.* London: Metheun & Co. Ltd, 1970.

Fulton, Bruce. "The Boulanger Affair Revisited: The Preservation of the Third Republic, 1889." *French Historical Studies* 17.2 (Autumn, 1991): 310–29.

Geary, Dick, ed. *Labour and Socialist Movements in Europe before 1914.* Providence: Berg Publishers, 1989.

———. "Socialism, Revolution and the European Labour Movement, 1848–1918." *The Historical Journal* 15.4 (Dec., 1972): 794–803.

Geffroy, Gustave. *L'Enfermé: Avec Le Masque de Blanqui,* Paris: Bibliothèque Charpentier, 1919.

Gluckstein, Donny. *The Paris Commune: A Revolution in Democracy.* Chicago: Haymarket Books, 2011.

Greene, Doug Enaa. "Blanqui, Benjamin, and the Politics of the Apocalypse." *Red Wedge.* http://www.redwedgemagazine.com/online-issue/benjamin -blanqui-and-the-apocalypse0.

———. "Bullets and Barricades: On the Art of Insurrection." *LINKS International Journal of Socialist Renewal.* http://links.org.au/barricades-bullets -insurrection-revolution.

———. "At the Crossroads of Blanquism and Leninism." *LINKS International Journal of Socialist Renewal.* http://links.org.au/node/4708.

———. "Day of the People: Gracchus Babeuf and the Communist Idea." *LINKS International Journal of Socialist Renewal.* http://links.org.au/ node/3228.

———. "The First Words of Common Sense: A Closer Look at Blanquism." The Blanquist. https://blanquist.blogspot.com/2017/07/the-first-words -of-common-sense-closer.html.

———. "The final aim is nothing: The politics of revisionism and anti-revisionism." *LINKS International Journal of Socialist Renewal.* http://links .org.au/node/4677.

———. "Leninism and Blanquism." *Cultural Logic* (2012). http://clogic. eserver.org/2012/Greene.pdf

———. "Leon Trotsky and revolutionary insurrection." *LINKS International Journal of Socialist Renewal.* http://links.org.au/node/3637.

———. "The Rise of Marxism in France." *LINKS International Journal of Socialist Renewal.* http://links.org.au/node/4684.

———. "The will to act: The life and thought of Louis-Auguste Blanqui." *LINKS International Journal of Socialist Renewal.* http://links.org.au/ node/4115.

Guérin, Daniel, ed. *No Gods, No Masters.* Oakland: AK Press, 2005.

Hallward, Peter. "Blanqui's Bifurcations." *Radical Philosophy* 185 (May-June

2014): 36–44.

Harman, Chris. *A People's History of the World: From the Stone Age to the New Millennium.* New York: Verso Books, 2008.

Harsin, Jill. *Barricades: The War of the Streets in Revolutionary Paris, 1830–1848.* New York: Palgrave Macmillan, 2002.

Harvey, David. *Capital of Modernity.* New York: Routledge Books, 2006.

Haynes, Mike, and Jim Wolfreys, ed., *History and Revolution: Refuting Revisionism.* New York: Verso Books, 2007.

Hazan, Eric. *A History of the Barricade.* New York: Verso, 2015.

———. *The Invention of Paris: A History in Footsteps.* New York: Verso, 2010.

———. *A People's History of the French Revolution.* New York: Verso, 2014.

Hobsbawm, Eric. *The Age of Revolution 1789–1848.* New York: Vintage Books, 1996.

———. *Primitive Rebels: Studies in Archaic Forms of Social Movements in the 19th and 20th Centuries.* New York: W. W. Norton & Company, 1965.

Horne, Alistair. *The Fall of Paris: The Siege and the Commune 1870–71.* New York: Penguin Books, 1990.

Howorth, Patrick. "The Myth of Blanquism under the Third Republic." *Journal of Modern History* 48.3 (Sept. 1976): 37–68.

Hugo, Victor. *Memoirs of Victor Hugo.* London: William Heineman, 1899.

Hunt, Richard. *The Political Ideas of Marx and Engels I: Marxism and Totalitarian Democracy, 1818–1850.* Pittsburgh: University of Pittsburgh Press, 1974.

———. *The Political Ideas of Marx and Engels II: Classical Marxism, 1850–1895.* Pittsburgh: University of Pittsburgh Press, 1984.

Hutton, Patrick H. *The Cult of Revolutionary Tradition: The Blanquists in French Politics, 1864–1893.* Berkeley: University of California Press, 1981.

———. "Popular Boulangism and the Advent of Mass Politics in France, 1886–90." *Journal of Contemporary History* 11.1 (Jan., 1976): 85–106.

———. "The Role of the Blanquist Party in Left-Wing Politics in France, 1879–1890." *The Journal of Modern History* 46.2 (June, 1974): 277–95.

Irvine, William D. *The Boulanger Affair Reconsidered: Royalism, Boulangism, and the Origins of the Radical Right in France.* New York: Oxford University Press, 1989.

Jellinek, Frank. *The Paris Commune of 1871.* New York: Grosset and Dunlap, 1965.

Johnstone, Monty. "Marx, Blanqui and Majority Rule." *Socialist Register* (1983): 296–318.

Judt, Tony. *Marxism and the French Left: Studies on Labour and Politics in France 1830–1982.* New York: New York University Press, 2011.

Kautsky, Karl. "Terrorism and Communism," *Marxists Internet Archive.* http://www.marxistsfr.org/archive/kautsky/1919/terrcomm/index.htm.

Kouvelakis, Stathis. *Philosophy and Revolution: From Kant to Marx*. New York: Verso Books, 2003.

Lefebvre, Georges. *The French Revolution: Volume I from Its Origins to 1793*. New York: Routledge, 1962.

———. *The French Revolution: Volume II from 1793 to 1799*. New York: Columbia University Press, 1964.

———. *Napoleon: From 18th Brumaire to Tilsit 1799–1807*. New York: Columbia University Press, 1969.

———. *Napoleon: From Tilsit to Waterloo 1807–1815*. New York: Columbia University Press, 1969.

Lenin, Vladimir Ilyich. *V. I. Lenin Collected Works: 45 Volumes*. Moscow: Progress Publishers, 1974.

Lissagaray, Pierre-Olivier. *History of the Paris Commune of 1871*. St. Petersburg, Florida: Red and Black Publishers, 2007.

Luxemburg, Rosa. *Essential Rosa Luxemburg*. Chicago: Haymarket Books, 2008.

Marty, André. "Figuras do Movimento Operário: Alguns Aspectos da Atividade de Blanqui," *Marxists Internet Archive*. https://www.marxists.org/portugues/marty/1951/02/06.htm.

Marx, Karl, and Frederick Engels. *The Birth of the Communist Manifesto*. Edited by Dirk Struik. New York: International Publishers, 1993.

———. *The Collected Works of Karl Marx and Frederick Engels: 50 Volumes*. London: Lawrence & Wishart, 1975.

Mason, Edward S. "Blanqui and Communism." *Political Science Quarterly* 44.4 (Dec., 1929), 498–527.

Mason, Paul. *Live Working or Die Fighting: How the Working Class Went Global*. Chicago: Haymarket Books, 2007.

Mayer, Arno J. *The Furies: Violence and Terror in the French and Russian Revolutions*. Princeton: Princeton University Press, 2000.

Mazgaj, Paul. "The Origins of the French Radical Right: A Historiographical Essay." *French Historical Studies* 15.2 (Autumn, 1987): 287–315.

Molinier, Sylvain. *Blanqui*. Paris: Presses universitaires de France, 1948.

Molyneux, John. *Marxism and the Party*. Chicago: Haymarket Books, 2003.

Mooers, Colin. *The Making of Bourgeois Europe*. Verso: New York, 1991.

Mosse, George L. "The French Right and the Working Classes: Les Jaunes." *Journal of Contemporary History* 7.3 (July-Oct., 1972): 185-208;

Neuberg, A. *Armed Insurrection*. New York: St. Martin's, 1970.

Rancière, Jacques. *Proletarian Nights: The Workers' Dream in Nineteenth Century France*. New York: Verso Books, 2012.

———. "The Radical Gap: A Preface to Auguste Blanqui, *Eternity by the Stars*." *Radical Philosophy* 185 (May-June 2014): 19–25.

Riazanov, David. "The Relations of Marx and Blanqui," *Marxists Internet Archive*. http://www.marxists.org/archive/riazanov/1928/xx/blanqui.htm.

Robertson, Priscilla. *Revolutions of 1848: A Social History*. Princeton: Princeton University Press, 1962.

Schulkind, Eugene, ed. *The Paris Commune of 1871: The View from the Left*. New York: Grove Press, 1974.

Sewell, William. *Work and Revolution in France 1789-1848*. Cambridge: Cambridge University Press, 1980.

Slavin, Morris. *The Left and the French Revolution*. Atlantic Highlands: Humanities Press, 1995.

Soboul, Albert. *The French Revolution 1787–1799: From the Storming of the Bastille to Napoleon*. New York: Vintage Books, 1975.

———. *The Sans-Culottes*. Princeton: Princeton University Press, 1978.

Spitzer, Alan. *Old Hatreds and Young Hopes: The French Carbonari against the Bourbon Restoration*. Cambridge: Harvard University Press, 1971.

———. *The Revolutionary Theories of Louis-Auguste Blanqui*. New York: Columbia University Press, 1957.

Steenson, Gary. *After Marx, Before Lenin: Marxism and Socialist Working Class Parties in Europe, 1884–1914*. Pittsburgh: University of Pittsburgh Press, 1991.

Stuart, Robert. *Marxism at Work: Ideology, class and French socialism during the Third Republic*. New York: Cambridge University Press, 1992.

Thomas, Edith. *The Women Incendiaries*. Chicago: Haymarket Books, 2007.

Tocqueville, Alexis de. *Recollections of Tocqueville*. New York: The MacMillan Co., 1896.

Tombs, Robert. *The Paris Commune 1871*. New York: Longman, 1999.

Traugott, Mark. *Armies of the Poor: Determinants of Working-Class Participation in the Parisian Insurrection of June 1848*. Princeton: Princeton University Press, 1985.

———. *The Insurgent Barricade*. Berkeley: University of California Press, 2010.

Trotsky, Leon. *History of the Russian Revolution*. Ann Arbor: University of Michigan Press, 1967.

———. *Problems of the Chinese Revolution*. Ann Arbor: University of Michigan Press, 1967.

NOTES

INTRODUCTION

1. Louis-Auguste Blanqui, "Communism, the Future of Society," *The Blanqui Archive*. https://blanqui.kingston.ac.uk/texts/communism -the-future-of-society-1869/.

I. BEGINNINGS

1. Albert Soboul, *The Sans-Culottes* (Princeton: Princeton University Press, 1978), 256–57.
2. See Georges Lefebvre, *The French Revolution: Volume I from Its Origins to 1793*, (New York: Routledge, 1962); Georges Lefebvre, *The French Revolution: Volume II from 1793 to 1799* (New York: Columbia University Press, 1964); Georges Lefebvre, *Napoleon: From 18th Brumaire to Tilsit 1799–1807* (New York: Columbia University Press, 1969); Georges Lefebvre, *Napoleon: From Tilsit to Waterloo 1807–1815* (New York: Columbia University Press, 1969); Albert Soboul, *The French Revolution 1787–1799: From the Storming of the Bastille to Napoleon* (New York: Vintage Books, 1975); Eric Hazan, *A People's History of the French Revolution* (New York: Verso, 2014); Morris Slavin, *The Left and the French Revolution* (Atlantic Highlands: Humanities Press, 1995); Issac Deutscher, *Stalin* (New York: Penguin Books, 1977), 539–40.
3. Quoted in Mike Haynes and Jim Wolfreys, ed., *History and Revolution: Refuting Revisionism* (New York: Verso Books, 2007), 58.
4. Sources for most of this section can be found in Samuel Bernstein, *Louis-Auguste Blanqui and the Art of Insurrection* (London: Lawrence and Wishart, 1971), 14–25.
5. Quoted in Philippe Le Goff and Peter Hallward, "Chronology," *The Blanqui Archive*. http://www.fiveeightsix.co.uk/blanqui.kingston.ac.uk /chronology/.
6. Cited in Maurice Dommanget, *Blanqui* (Paris: Études et documentation internationales, 1970), 1.

167

7. Bernstein 1971, 23.
8. Cited in Dommanget 1970, 1.

II. COMMITMENT

1. Quoted in Michel Beaud, *A History of Capitalism 1500–1980* (New York: Monthly Review Press, 1983), 94.
2. See Arno J. Mayer, *The Furies: Violence and Terror in the French and Russian Revolutions* (Princeton: Princeton University Press, 2000), 583–91; Alan Spitzer, *Old Hatreds and Young Hopes: The French Carbonari against the Bourbon Restoration* (Cambridge: Harvard University Press, 1971), 23–24, 281–82, 290–91, 294–95.
3. Ibid., 279.
4. Ibid., 290.
5. Ibid., 241.
6. Ibid., 77–141.
7. Ibid., 173–74. For more on the four sergeants of Rochelle, see ibid., 125–28.
8. Ibid., 174.
9. Ibid., 178.
10. "Chronology"; Bernstein 1971, 25.
11. Bernstein 1971, 26; Spitzer 1971, 261 and 264.
12. Gustave Geffroy, *L'Enfermé: Avec le Masque de Blanqui* (Paris: Bibliothèque Charpentier, 1919), 36.
13. Spitzer 1971, 93.
14. Ibid., 26–7; William J. Fishman, *The Insurrectionists* (London: Metheun & Co. Ltd, 1970), 58.
15. Mayer 2000, 596–97.
16. Ibid., 29.
17. "Chronology."
18. Quoted in Bernstein 1971, 30.
19. "Chronology."
20. Ibid.
21. Bernstein 1971, 53.
22. "Communism, the Future of Society."
23. Louis-Auguste Blanqui, "Notes on Positivism," *Marxists Internet Archive.* https://www.marxists.org/reference/archive/blanqui/1869/positivism.htm.
24. Bernstein 1971, 273.
25. Ibid.
26. Ibid.
27. Blanqui, "The Sects and the Revolution," *The Blanqui Archive.* https://blanqui.kingston.ac.uk/texts/the-sects-and-the-revolution-19-october

-1866/; Louis-Auguste Blanqui, *Critique Sociale Volume 2: Fragments et notes* (Paris: Félix Alcan, 1885b), 113.

28. Quoted in Spitzer, *The Revolutionary Theories of Louis-Auguste Blanqui* (New York: Columbia University Press, 1957), 82.

29. Quoted in Bernstein 1971, 32.

30. Spitzer 1971, 7, 277, 292.

31. Quoted in Stathis Kouvelakis, *Philosophy and Revolution: From Kant to Marx* (New York: Verso Books, 2003), 85.

32. For more on Saint-Simonism, see Samuel Bernstein, "Saint-Simon's Philosophy of History," in *Essays in Political and Intellectual History* (New York: Paine-Whitman Publishers, 1955), 100–12.

33. Quoted in Walter Benjamin, *The Arcades Project* (Cambridge: Harvard University Press, 1999), 736.

34. Quoted in Spitzer 1957, 105.

35. Louis-Auguste Blanqui, *Critique Sociale, volume 1 Capital et travail* (Paris: Félix Alcan, 1885a), 196 and 201.

36. Quoted in Spitzer 1957, 108; Blanqui 1885b, 314.

37. Blanqui 1885a, 193; Blanqui 1885b, 113.

38. Louis-Auguste Blanqui, "Social Wealth Must Belong to Those Who Created It," *The Blanqui Archive.* https://blanqui.kingston.ac.uk/texts /social-wealth-must-belong-to-those-who-created-it-february-1834/; Spitzer 1957, 51–52.

39. Jill Harsin, *Barricades: The War of the Streets in Revolutionary Paris, 1830–1848* (New York: Palgrave Macmillan, 2002), 40.

40. Ibid.

41. Quoted in Bernstein 1971, 33.

42. Ibid., 33.

43. Ibid., 34.

44. Quoted in ibid.

45. Spitzer 1971, 5.

46. Louis-Auguste Blanqui, "Call to Arms," *Marxists Internet Archive.* https://www.marxists.org/reference/archive/blanqui/1830/appel -aux-armes.htm.

47. Bernstein 1971, 36.

48. Harsin 2002, 41.

49. Louis-Auguste Blanqui, "Speech before the Society of the Friends of the People," *Marxists Internet Archive*, marxists.org/reference/archive /blanqui/1832/speech.htm.

III. The Underground

1. *Marx and Engels Collected Works*, vol. 10, "The Class Struggles in France, 1848–1850," (London: Lawrence and Wishart, 1975), 48. (henceforth

MECW).

2. Ibid. 50.
3. *MECW,* vol. 4, "The Holy Family," 124.
4. Bernstein 1971, 42.
5. Ibid.
6. Harsin 2002, 49.
7. Louis-Auguste Blanqui, "Appeal to the Students," *Marxists Internet Archive.* https://www.marxists.org/reference/archive/blanqui/1830/appeal-students.htm.
8. Bernstein 1971, 43.
9. Louis-Auguste Blanqui, "Declaration of the Provisional Committee for Schools," *The Blanqui Archive.* https://blanqui.kingston.ac.uk/texts/declaration-of-the-provisional-committee-for-schools-22-january-1831/.
10. Arthur L. Dunham, "Industrial Life and Labor in France 1815–1848," *Journal of Economic History* 3.3 (November 1943): 124; Tony Judt, *Marxism and the French Left: Studies on Labour and Politics in France 1830–1982* (New York: New York University Press, 2011), 31–37; Colin Mooers, *The Making of Bourgeois Europe* (Verso: New York, 1991), 83.
11. Wolfgang Abendroth, *A Short History of the European Working Class* (New York: Monthly Review Press, 1972), 13–14.
12. Mooers 1991, 80; Geoff Eley, *Forging Democracy: The History of the Left in Europe, 1850–2000* (New York: Oxford University Press, 2002), 14–15.
13. Quoted in Benjamin 1999, 24–25.
14. Quoted in William Sewell, *Work and Revolution in France 1789–1848* (Cambridge: Cambridge University Press, 1980), 198.
15. Robert J. Bezucha, *The Lyon Uprising of 1834: Social and Political Conflict in the Early July Monarchy* (Cambridge: Harvard University Press, 1974); Paul Mason, *Live Working or Die Fighting: How the Working Class Went Global* (Chicago: Haymarket Books, 2007), 32–49.
16. Harsin 2002, 49–50; Bernstein 1971, 44.
17. Harsin 2002, 49; Bernstein 1971, 46.
18. Quoted in Benjamin 1999, 735.
19. Louis-Auguste Blanqui, "Defense speech at the 'Trial of the Fifteen,'" *Marxists Internet Archive.* https://www.marxists.org/reference/archive/blanqui/1832/defence-speech.htm. Unless otherwise noted, all emphasis is that of Blanqui.
20. Ibid.
21. Ibid.
22. Ibid.
23. Ibid.

24. Ibid.
25. Ibid.
26. Ibid.
27. Ibid.
28. Ibid.
29. Ibid.
30. Ibid.
31. Ibid.
32. Ibid.
33. Bernstein 1971, 48.
34. Louis-Auguste Blanqui, "Letter to Maillard," *The Blanqui Archive*. https:// blanqui.kingston.ac.uk/texts/letter-to-maillard-belle-ile-6-june-1852/.
35. Louis-Auguste Blanqui, "Speech before the Society of the Friends of the People," *Marxists Internet Archive*. https://www.marxists.org/reference /archive/blanqui/1832/speech.htm.
36. Ibid.
37. Ibid.
38. Ibid.
39. Ibid.
40. Ibid.
41. Ibid.
42. Ibid.
43. Ibid.
44. Ibid.
45. Ibid.
46. Ibid.
47. Louis-Auguste Blanqui, "First issue of *Le Libérateur*," *Marxists Internet Archive*. https://www.marxists.org/reference/archive/blanqui/1834 /liberateur.htm.
48. "Social Wealth Must Belong to Those Who Created It."
49. Ibid.
50. Ibid.
51. Ibid.
52. Ibid.
53. Ibid.
54. Ibid.
55. Ibid.
56. Ibid.
57. Ibid.
58. Louis-Auguste Blanqui, "Equality Is Our Flag," *The Blanqui Archive*. https:// blanqui.kingston.ac.uk/texts/equality-is-our-flag-2-february-1834/.

59. "Social Wealth Must Belong to Those Who Created It."
60. Ibid.
61. "Equality Is Our Flag."
62. Louis-Auguste Blanqui, "Democratic Propaganda," *The Blanqui Archive.* https://blanqui.kingston.ac.uk/texts/democratic-propaganda-1835/.
63. Louis-Auguste Blanqui, "Why There Are No More Riots," *The Blanqui Archive.* https://blanqui.kingston.ac.uk/texts/why-there-are-no-more-riots-2-february-1834/.
64. "Democratic Propaganda."
65. Blanqui 1885b, 146.
66. Bernstein 1971, 52.
67. Harsin 2002, 65–75.
68. Ian Birchall, *The Spectre of Babeuf* (Chicago: Haymarket, 2016); Doug Enaa Greene, "Day of the people: Gracchus Babeuf and the communist idea," *LINKS International Journal of Socialist Renewal.* http://links.org.au/node/3228.
69. Birchall 2016, 195.
70. Ibid.
71. Philippe Buonarroti, History of Babeuf's Conspiracy for Equality (London: H. Hetherinton, 1836), 72 and 24.
72. Elizabeth Eisenstein, *The First Professional Revolutionist: Filippo Buonarroti (1761–1837)* (Cambridge: Harvard University Press, 1959), 28–80; Spitzer 1957, 267, 269–72.
73. Birchall 2016, 101.
74. Spitzer 1957, 126; Eisenstein 1959, 126.
75. Buonarroti 1836, 66.
76. Ibid., 65, 74, 107–10.
77. "Why There Are No More Riots."
78. Bernstein 1971, 71.
79. Harsin 2002, 112.
80. Ibid., 106.
81. Quoted in ibid., 114. See also Eric Hobsbawm, *Primitive Rebels: Studies in Archaic Forms of Social Movements in the 19th and 20ᵗʰ Centuries* (New York: W. W. Norton & Company, 1965), 193.
82. Harsin 2002, 111; Louis-Auguste Blanqui, "Organization of the Society of Families," *Marxists Internet Archive.* https://www.marxists.org/reference/archive/blanqui/1834/families.htm.
83. Bernstein 1971, 73.
84. "Letter to Maillard."
85. Louis-Auguste Blanqui, "Work, Suffer, and Die," *The Blanqui Archive.* https://blanqui.kingston.ac.uk/texts/work-suffer-and-die-c-1851-52/.

86. Bernstein 1971, 75.

87. Harsin 2002, 115–16.

88. Louis-Auguste Blanqui, "Blanqui's Notes for His Defence at the 'Gunpowder Trial,'" *The Blanqui Archive*. https://blanqui.kingston.ac.uk/texts/blanquis-notes-for-his-defence-at-the-gunpowder-trial-october-1836/.

89. Ibid.

90. Ibid.

91. Ibid.

92. Ibid.

IV. Aux Armes!

1. Bernstein 1971, 77.

2. Ibid., 79.

3. Harsin 2002, 119.

4. Bernstein 1971, 80.

5. Bernstein 77–78. See Karl Marx and Frederick Engels, *The Birth of the Communist Manifesto*, edited by Dirk Struik (New York: International Publishers, 1993), 56–62.

6. Harsin 2002, 120.

7. Ibid., 118.

8. Bernstein 1971, 95.

9. Quoted in Harsin 2002, 137.

10. Bernstein 1971, 74–75.

11. Louis-Auguste Blanqui, "Reception Procedure of the Society of the Seasons," *Marxists Internet Archive*. https://www.marxists.org/reference/archive/blanqui/1830/seasons.htm.

12. Ibid.

13. Bernstein 1971, 86.

14. Ibid., 87.

15. Quoted in Spitzer 1957, 160.

16. Bernstein 1971, 88.

17. Louis-Auguste Blanqui, "Appeal of the Committee of the Society of the Seasons," *Marxists Internet Archive*. https://www.marxists.org/reference/archive/blanqui/1839/appeal.htm.

18. Bernstein 1971, 91.

19. Harsin 2002, 125.

20. Bernstein 1971, 93–97; Harsin 2002, 137–41; Alain Decaux, *Blanqui, L'Insurgé: La Passion de la révolution* (Paris: Librairie académique Perrin, 1976), 210–11.

V. L'Enfermé

1. Quoted in "Chronology."

2. Bernstein 1971, 100–101; Harsin 2002, 233–44; Geffroy 1919, 95.
3. Harsin 2002, 240.
4. Geffroy 1919, 230–31; Patrick Hutton, *The Cult of Revolutionary Tradition: The Blanquists in French Politics, 1864–1893* (Berkeley: University of California Press, 1981), 23.
5. Bernstein 1971, 102 and 246.
6. Quoted in Harsin 2002, 236.
7. Ibid., 240 and 244–46.
8. Quoted in ibid. 243; Bernstein 1971, 105.
9. Fishman 1970, 66.
10. Bernstein 1971, 94.
11. Ibid., 114.
12. Spitzer 1957, 7–8.

VI. 1848

1. Bernstein 1971, 119; Eric Hobsbawm, *The Age of Revolution 1789–1848* (New York: Vintage Books, 1996), 307; Harsin 2002, 251–74.
2. Alexis de Tocqueville, *Recollections of Tocqueville* (New York: The MacMillan Co., 1896), 92–94.
3. *MECW*, vol. 10, "The Class Struggles in France, 1848–1850," 54–55.
4. Benjamin 1999, 177; Harsin 2002, 278. Although clubs shielding Bonapartist and monarchists existed, the police spent their time keeping a careful watch on socialist and revolutionary clubs.
5. Louis Blanc quoted in Donny Gluckstein, *The Paris Commune: A Revolution in Democracy* (Chicago: Haymarket Books, 2011), 182.
6. Harman, *A People's History of the World* (New York: Verso Books, 2008), 339.
7. *MECW*, vol. 10, "The Class Struggles in France, 1848–1850," 61.
8. See Samuel Bernstein, "Marx in Paris, 1848: A Neglected Chapter," *Science & Society* 3.3 (Summer 1939): 340.
9. Louis-Auguste Blanqui, "To the Democratic Clubs of Paris," *Marxists Internet Archive.* https://www.marxists.org/reference/archive/blanqui/1848/democratic-clubs.htm.
10. Louis-Auguste Blanqui, "For the Red Flag," *Marxists Internet Archive.* https://www.marxists.org/reference/archive/blanqui/1848/red-flag.htm.
11. Louis-Auguste Blanqui, "Speech at the Prado," *The Blanqui Archive.* https://blanqui.kingston.ac.uk/texts/speech-at-the-prado-25-february-1848/.
12. Bernstein 1971, 136.
13. Victor Hugo, *Memoirs of Victor Hugo* (London: William Heineman, 1899), 292.
14. Bernstein 1971, 146.
15. For the full list of demands in the petition see Louis-Auguste Blanqui,

"Address of Central Republican Society to the Government," *Marxists Internet Archive*. https://www.marxists.org/reference/archive/blanqui /1848/republican-society.htm; Spitzer 1957, 85.

16. Louis-Auguste Blanqui, "Warning to the People," *Marxists Internet Archive*. https://www.marxists.org/reference/archive/blanqui/1851 /toast.htm.

17. Ibid.

18. Ibid.

19. Spitzer 1957, 140.

20. Bernstein 1971, 147.

21. Louis-Auguste Blanqui, "Second Petition for the Postponing of Elections," *The Blanqui Archive*. https://blanqui.kingston.ac.uk/texts /second-petition-for-the-postponing-of-elections-14-march-1848/.

22. Bernstein 1971, 149.

23. Ibid. 151.

24. *MECW*, vol. 10, "The Class Struggles in France, 1848–1850," 127.

25. Bernstein 1971, 158.

26. Ibid., 159.

27. For conflicting accounts on the Taschereau Document, see Dommanget 1970, 12–16; Geffroy 1919, 147–54; Bernstein 1971, 107, 158; Decaux 1976, 315–48.

28. Harsin 2002, 285.

29. Louis-Auguste Blanqui, "Blanqui's Response to the Tascherau Document," *Marxists Internet Archive*. https://www.marxists.org/reference /archive/blanqui/1848/tascherau.htm.

30. Ibid.

31. Ibid.

32. Ibid.

33. Ibid.

34. Bernstein 1971, 161.

35. Ibid., 163.

36. Ibid., 168–69.

37. Harsin 2002, 284; and Bernstein 1971, 171.

38. Louis-Auguste Blanqui, "The Central Republican Society," *Marxists Internet Archive*. https://www.marxists.org/reference/archive/blanqui /1848/central-republican-society.htm.

39. Bernstein 1971, 178; Harsin 2002, 288.

40. Tocqueville 1896, 163.

41. Harsin 2002, 287–93.

42. Ibid., 29–318.

43. *MECW*, vol. 11, "The 18th Brumaire of Louis Bonaparte," 110.

VII. THE MOUNTAIN IS DEAD

1. Bernstein 1971, 190.
2. Sylvain Molinier, *Blanqui* (Paris: Presses universitaires de France, 1948), 47; Michael Elliott-Bateman, John Ellis, and Tom Bowden, ed., *Revolt to Revolution: Studies in the 19th and 20th Century European Experience*, Fourth Dimension of Warfare: Vol. 2 (Manchester: Manchester University Press, 1974), 76.
3. Quoted in Eric Hazan, *The Invention of Paris: A History in Footsteps* (New York: Verso, 2010), 266.
4. Bernstein 1971, 201.
5. Ibid., 209–12 and 216–18.
6. See *MECW*, vol. 10, "Introduction to the Leaflet of L. A. Blanqui's Toast Sent to the Refugee Committee 1851," 537; Hal Draper, *Karl Marx's Theory of Revolution Volume 3: The "Dictatorship of the Proletariat"* (New York: Monthly Review Press: 1986), 128–29.
7. "Warning to the People."
8. Ibid.
9. Bernstein 1971, 156–57.
10. Louis-Auguste Blanqui, "To the Mountain of 1793! To the Pure Socialists, Its True Heirs!" *Marxists Internet Archive*. https://www.marxists.org/reference/archive/blanqui/1849/to-mountain.htm.
11. Ibid.
12. Ibid.
13. Ibid.
14. "Work, Suffer and Die."
15. Ibid.
16. "To the Mountain of 1793! To the Pure Socialists, Its True Heirs!"
17. Louis-Auguste Blanqui, "Philosophical and Political Fragments," *The Blanqui Archive*. https://blanqui.kingston.ac.uk/texts/fragments-philosophiques-et-politiques-1840s-70s/.
18. Bernstein 1971, 272–73.
19. "Letter to Maillard."
20. Ibid.
21. Ibid.
22. Hal Draper, *Karl Marx's Theory of Revolution Volume 1: State and Bureaucracy* (New York: Monthly Review Press, 1977), 386.
23. *MECW*, vol. 22, "The Civil War in France," 330.
24. Quoted in Benjamin 1999, 136.
25. *MECW*, vol. 11, "The 18th Brumaire of Louis Bonaparte," 187–88.
26. Ibid., 150.
27. Ibid.
28. Quoted in Gluckstein 2011, 53.

29. Ibid., 53.
30. *MECW*, vol. 22, "The Civil War in France," 330.
31. Mooers 1991, 88; David Harvey, *Paris, Capital of Modernity* (New York: Routledge Books, 2006), 109.
32. Frank Jellinek, *The Paris Commune of 1871* (New York: Grosset and Dunlap, 1965), 34.
33. Gluckstein 2011, 53.
34. Harvey 2006, 165–66.
35. Benjamin 1999, 12.
36. *MECW*, vol. 11. "The 18th Brumaire of Louis Bonaparte," 185–86.
37. Louis-Auguste Blanqui, "Letter to Tessy," *The Blanqui Archive*. https:// blanqui.kingston.ac.uk/texts/letter-to-tessy-belle-ile-6-september-1852/.
38. Ibid.
39. Ibid.
40. Ibid.
41. Ibid.
42. Ibid.
43. Spitzer 1957, 120.
44. *MECW*, vol. 13, "The Sevastopol Hoax—General News, Oct. 6, 1854," 491.
45. Quoted in Bernstein 1971, 235.
46. Spitzer 1957, 152–53.
47. See also Maurice Dommanget, "La vie de Blanqui sous le Second Empire: De la Sortie de Belle-Île a la Sortie de Sainte-Pélagie (1er Decembre 1857–12 Mars 1864)," *Le Mouvement social*, No. 35 (Apr.–Jun., 1961): 30–41.
48. Quoted in Bernstein 1971, 248.
49. Quoted in ibid.
50. Ibid., 252.
51. Quoted in ibid.
52. Ibid., 253.
53. *MECW*, vol. 41, "Karl Marx to Ferdinand Lassalle–July 22, 1861," 318.
54. Bernstein 1971, 256.
55. Ibid., 255.
56. Quoted in Leslie Derfler, *Paul Lafargue and the Founding of French Marxism, 1842–1882* (Cambridge, MA: Harvard University Press, 1991), 28–29.
57. See Bernstein 1971, 260–61; Hutton 1981, 41–42.

VIII. The Duty of a Revolutionary

1. Bernstein 1971, 282.
2. Hutton 1981, 10–11.
3. The police forces of the Second Empire believed that the Blanquists contained no more than 3,000 members. Higher figures range from

6,000 to 7,000. See Bernstein 1971, 283–84. Gluckstein gives a much lower figure of 800 in 1868. See 2011, 67. Spitzer (1957, 153) gives a figure of approximately 2,000.

4. Hutton 1981, 24.
5. Bernstein 1971, 284.
6. Spitzer 1957, 165–66.
7. Draper 1986, 126–27; Charles da Costa, *Les Blanquistes* (Paris: Librairie des Sciences Politiques et Sociales, 1912), 19.
8. Bernstein 1971, 288.
9. Mason 1929, 520.
10. Spitzer 1957, 140–41.
11. Hutton 1981, 29.
12. Pierre-Joseph Proudhon, "Property Is Theft," in *No Gods, No Masters*, ed. Daniel Guérin (Oakland: AK Press, 2005), 48–54.
13. Bernstein 1971, 292–93.
14. Samuel Bernstein, *The Beginnings of Marxian Socialism in France* (New York: Russell & Russell, 1965), 32.
15. Bernstein 1971, 294–96 and Hutton 1981, 28.
16. *MECW*, vol. 43, "Marx to Engels–March 1, 1869," 225.
17. Hutton 1981, 38.
18. Ibid., 40.
19. Ibid., 41.
20. Spitzer 1957, 81.
21. Hutton 1981, 28.
22. Ibid., 49.
23. Ibid.
24. Ibid.
25. Ibid., 52.
26. Ibid.
27. "Philosophical and Political Fragments."
28. Hutton 1981, 52.
29. Ibid., 54.
30. Ibid., 42–43.
31. Bernstein 1971, 285.
32. Quoted in Benjamin 1999, 618.
33. Bernstein 1971, 308–9.
34. "Communism, the Future of Society."
35. Louis-Auguste Blanqui, "Instructions for an Armed Uprising," *The Blanqui Archive*. https://blanqui.kingston.ac.uk/texts/instructions-for-an-armed-uprising-1868/.
36. Ibid.

37. Ibid.
38. Ibid.
39. Ibid.
40. Ibid.
41. Ibid.; Dommanget 1970, 68–71.
42. "Instructions for an Armed Uprising."
43. "Communism, the Future of Society."
44. Bernstein 1971, 311.
45. "Communism, the Future of Society."
46. Eric Hazan, *A History of the Barricade* (New York: Verso, 2015), 124; Doug Enaa Greene, "Bullets and Barricades: On the Art of Insurrection," *LINKS International Journal of Socialist Renewal.* http://links.org.au /barricades-bullets-insurrection-revolution; Doug Enaa Greene, "The First Words of Common Sense: A Closer Look at Blanquism." The Blanquist. https://blanquist.blogspot.com/2017/07/the-first-words-of-common-sense-closer.html..
47. "Notes on Positivism."
48. Ibid.
49. Ibid.
50. Geffroy 1919, 239.
51. Ibid., 62.
52. Walter Benjamin, *Walter Benjamin: Selected Writings: Volume 4, 1938–1940*, ed. Howard Eiland and Michael W. Jennings (Cambridge: Harvard University Press, 2003), 188.
53. Quoted in Louis-Auguste Blanqui, *Maintenant, il faut des armes*, ed. Dominique Le Nuz (Paris: La Fabrique éditions, 2006), 25.
54. "Instructions for an Armed Uprising."
55. Geffroy 1919, 276–77.
56. Jellinek 1965, 49–52.
57. Ibid., 57.
58. Spitzer 1957, 154.
59. Benjamin 1999, 143.
60. Quoted in Gluckstein 2011, 68.

IX. War and Revolution

1. *MECW*, vol. 22, "Second Address of the General Council of the International Working Men's Association on the Franco-Prussian War," 263.
2. Samuel Bernstein, *Essays in Political and Intellectual History* (New York: Paine-Whitman Publishers, 1955a), 144.
3. Bernstein 1971, 323.
4. Quoted in Mason 1929, 526.
5. Spitzer 1957, 121.

6. Spitzer 1957, 118; Blanqui 1885b, 73.
7. "Instructions for an Armed Uprising."
8. Quoted in Draper 1986, 275.
9. Mason 1929, 526.
10. Bernstein 1971, 324.
11. In 1793, France adopted a new calendar to symbolize its break with the *ancien régime*, which rectroactively began Year I with the foundation of the First Republic on September 22, 1792. According to the Republican Calendar, Year II lasted from September 22, 1793 to September 22, 1794. After thirteen years, the Revolutionary Calendar was abolished by Napoleon in 1805.
12. For more on the early leaders of the Third Republic see Gluckstein 2011, 79–80 and 82–83; Jellinek 1965, 61–63.
13. Robert Tombs, *The Paris Commune 1871* (New York: Longman, 1999), 47.
14. Louis-Auguste Blanqui "La Patrie en Danger," in *Communards: The Story of The Paris Commune of 1871 as Told by Those Who Fought for It*, ed. Mitchell Abidor (Pacifica, CA: Marxists Internet Archive, 2010), 40.
15. Bernstein 1971, 326.
16. Quoted in Gluckstein 2011, 96.
17. For an account of the coup attempt, see ibid., 96; Jellinek 1965, 78–79; Bernstein 1971, 327–28; Tombs 1999, 48–49.
18. Gluckstein 2011, 49.
19. "Chronology."
20. Tombs 1999, 58.
21. "The 'Red Poster' Issued by the Delegation of the Twenty Arrondisements," in *The Paris Commune of 1871: The View from the Left*, ed. Eugene Schulkind (New York: Grove Press, 1974), 85–86.
22. For information on the events surrounding the January 19 offensive, see Tombs 1999, 58–60.
23. Accounts of January 22 revolt can be found in Gluckstein 2011, 97–98; Jellinek 1965, 82–84; Bernstein 1971, 330.
24. Quoted from Gluckstein 2011, 98.
25. Louis-Auguste Blanqui, "One Last Word," *The Blanqui Archive*. https://blanqui.kingston.ac.uk/texts/one-last-word-12-february-1871/.
26. "Republican Committee of the Twenty Paris Arrondisements for National Defense" in *The Communards of Paris, 1871*, ed. Stewart Edwards (Ithaca: Cornell University Press, 1973), 44.
27. Ibid., 46.
28. Tombs 1999, 51.
29. Edith Thomas, *The Women Incendiaries* (Chicago: Haymarket Books, 2007), 38-9.

30. Gluckstein 2011, 86–87.
31. *MECW*, vol. 22, "Civil War in France," 330–31.
32. Pierre-Olivier Lissagaray, *History of the Paris Commune of 1871* (St. Petersburg, Florida: Red and Black Publishers, 2007), 62.
33. Ibid., 67.
34. Tombs 1999, 65.
35. Ibid., 67.
36. Lissagaray 2007, 72. See also Jellinek 1965, 109–26. Other firsthand accounts of the March 18th uprising can be found in Edwards 1973, 56–65. For the role of women in the March 18th revolution, see Thomas 2007, 52–69.
37. Gaston Da Costa, "The Commune Lived," in Abidor 2010, 173.
38. Hutton 1981, 72.
39. Ibid., 73.
40. Quoted in Gluckstein 2011, 117.
41. In actuality, no more than 30,000 National Guard were battle ready. See Alistair Horne, *The Fall of Paris: The Siege and the Commune 1870–71* (New York: Penguin Books, 1990), 329.
42. Ibid., 280.
43. For Duval's call for an immediate offensive, see Gluckstein 2010, 118; Lissagaray 2007, 163.
44. Horne 1990, 299–300.
45. Gaston Da Costa, "The Commune and Socialism," in Abidor 2010, 174–81.
46. Gluckstein 2011, 142; Draper 1986, 277–78.
47. Hutton 1981, 75.
48. Horne 1990, 300.
49. Ibid., 338.
50. *MECW*, vol. 22, "Civil War in France," 352.

X. Eternity by the Stars

1. Blanqui's *Eternity by the Stars* is a contested work. For different interpretations, see: Doug Enaa Greene, "Blanqui, Benjamin, and the Politics of the Apocalypse," *Red Wedge*. http://www.redwedgemagazine.com /online-issue/benjamin-blanqui-and-the-apocalypse0; Ian Birchall, "Why Did Walter Benjamin Misrepresent Blanqui?" *Grim and Dim.* http://grimanddim.org/historical-writings/2016-why-did-walter -benjamin-misrepresent-blanqui/; Bernstein 1971, 341–43; Spitzer 1957, 34–40; Hallward 2014, 36–44; Jacques Rancière, "The Radical Gap: A Preface to Auguste Blanqui, *Eternity by the Stars*," *Radical Philosophy* 185 (May-June 2014): 19–25; Daniel Bensaïd and Michael Löwy, "Auguste Blanqui, Heretical Communist," *Radical Philosophy* 185 (May-June 2014):

26–35.

2. Louis-Auguste Blanqui, *Eternity by the Stars* (New York: Contra Mundum Press, 2013), 113.
3. Ibid., 136.
4. Ibid., 125.
5. Decaux 1976, 594.

XI. Ni Dieu Ni Maître

1. Bernstein 1971, 342–43.
2. Samuel Bernstein, "Jules Guesde, Pioneer of Marxism in France," *Science & Society* 4.1 (Winter 1940b): 39.
3. Quoted in Bernstein 1971, 345.
4. Quoted in ibid., 348–49.
5. For the contents of the letter, see ibid., 349.
6. Draper 1986, 139. Draper adds the caveat that while Marx was interested in meeting Blanqui, he did not want him to lead the socialist party.
7. Bernstein 1971, 349–50; "Why Did Walter Benjamin Misrepresent Blanqui?" (note 398).
8. Spitzer 1957, 95.
9. Hutton 1981, 107–8.
10. Spitzer 1957, 17.

Conclusion: The Unconquered

1. "Communism, the Future of Society."

Appendix: Marxist Assessments of Blanqui

1. These conclusions are neatly summarized in Hal Draper, *Karl Marx's Theory of Revolution Volume 2: The Politics of Social Classes* (New York: Monthly Review Press, 1978), 40–48.
2. *MECW*, vol. 20, "Rules and Administrative Regulations of the International Workingmen's Association," 441.
3. *MECW*, vol. 41, "Marx to Louis Watteau–November 10, 1861," 326.
4. *MECW*, vol. 26, "History of the Communist League," 320.
5. *MECW*, vol. 10, "Address of the Central Committee to the Communist League (March Address)," 277–87.
6. *MECW*, vol. 10, "Meeting of the Central Authority September 15, 1850," 627.
7. John Molyneux, *Marxism and the Party* (Chicago: Haymarket Books, 2003), 22–23.
8. Richard Hunt, *The Political Ideas of Marx and Engels I: Marxism and Totalitarian Democracy, 1818–1850* (Pittsburgh: University of Pittsburgh Press, 1974), 249.

9. My conclusions are based heavily on Draper 1986, 184–213. The statutes of the SCUR are reprinted here from David Riazanov, "The Relations of Marx and Blanqui," *Marxists Internet Archive.* http://www .marxists.org/archive/riazanov/1928/xx/blanqui.htm.

10. Draper 1986, 210.

11. Ibid.

12. Spitzer 1957, 176.

13. See Draper 1986, 197; *MECW*, vol. 10, "K. Marx and F. Engels. A Letter to Adam, Barthélémy and Vidil – October 9, 1850," 484.

14. *MECW,* vol. 10, "Les Conspirateurs, par A. Chenu; ex-capitaine des gardes du citoyen Caussidière. Les societes secretes; la prefecture de police sous Caussidière; les corps-francs. La naissance de la Republique en fevrier 1848 par Lucien de la Hodde," 318.

15. *MECW*, vol. 23, "Introduction to Karl Marx's *Civil War in France*," 187.

16. *MECW,* vol. 24, "Programme of the Blanquist Commune Refugees," 13; Howorth, "The Myth of Blanquism under the Third Republic," *Journal of Modern History* 48.3 (Sept. 1976): 42.

17. Draper 1978, 559; Hunt 1974, 307–8.

18. Draper 1986, 281.

19. *MECW*, vol. 22, "Record of Marx's Speech on the Seventh Anniversary of the International [From the Newspaper Report on the Anniversary Meeting in London on September 24, 1871]," 634. These remarks of Marx were spoken at a banquet in September in 1871, meant as an anniversary celebration for the International. However what appears in *MECW* are not Marx's words per se, but actually a report from the banquet that was published in the *New York World.* While both Hunt and Draper are rightly skeptical of the reliability of the bourgeois press in this regard, both believe this report accurately conveys Marx's views on the dictatorship of the proletariat. Draper 1986, 292–95; Hunt 1974, 308–9.

20. Hutton 1981, 103.

21. Ibid.

22. Hunt 1974, 309.

23. Hutton 1981, 105.

24. *MECW,* vol. 24, "Programme of the Blanquist Commune Refugees," 13.

25. Ibid.16.

26. Walter Benjamin, "On the Concept of History" in *Illuminations* (New York: Schocken Books, 1968), 260.

27. See Doug Enaa Greene, "The final aim is nothing: The politics of revisionism and anti-revisionism," *LINKS International Journal of Socialist Renewal.* http://links.org.au/node/4677.

28. Eduard Bernstein, *The Preconditions of Socialism* (New York: University of Cambridge, 1993), 38–39.

29. Ibid., 46.

30. Rosa Luxemburg, *Essential Rosa Luxemburg* (Chicago: Haymarket Books, 2008), 89.

31. Karl Kautsky, "Terrorism and Communism," *Marxists Internet Archive.* https://www.marxists.org/archive/kautsky/1919/terrcomm/ch07.htm.

32. Maurice Dommanget, *Blanqui à Belle-Île* (Paris: Librairie du Travail, 1935), 7–11.

33. I have dealt at length with the relationship between Blanquism and Leninism elsewhere: Doug Enaa Greene, "Leninism and Blanquism," *Cultural Logic* (2012) http://clogic.eserver.org/2012/Greene.pdf; Doug Enaa Greene, "At the Crossroads of Blanquism and Leninism," *LINKS International Journal of Socialist Renewal.* http://links.org.au/node/4708.

34. *Lenin Collected Works*, vol. 25, "The Dual Power," (Moscow: Progress Publishers, 1974), 40. (henceforth *LCW*)

35. Leon Trotsky, *History of the Russian Revolution: Volume III Triumph of the Soviets* (Ann Arbor: University of Michigan Press, 1967), 170. For more on Trotsky and Blanqui on insurrection, see my "Leon Trotsky and revolutionary insurrection," *LINKS International Journal of Socialist Renewal.* http://links.org.au/node/3637.

36. *LCW*, vol. 26, "Marxism and Insurrection," 22–23.

37. A. Neuberg, *Armed Insurrection* (New York: St. Martin's, 1970), 42.

38. P. N. Fedoseyev, ed., *Scientific Communism* (Moscow: Progress Publishers, 1983), 46.

39. André Marty, "Figuras do Movimento Operário: Alguns Aspectos da Atividade de Blanqui," *Marxists Internet Archive.* https://www.marxists.org/portugues/marty/1951/02/06.htm; Spitzer 1957, 21–23.

40. Leon Trotsky, *Problems of the Chinese Revolution* (Ann Arbor: University of Michigan Press, 1967), 102.

INDEX

185

Also Available from Haymarket Books

Alexandra Kollontai: A Biography
Cathy Porter

Life and Death of Leon Trotsky
Natalia Ivanovna Sedova and Victor Serge,
Introduction by Richard Greeman

Lucy Parsons: An American Revolutionary
Carolyn Ashbaugh

The Old Man: John Brown at Harper's Ferry
Truman Nelson, Introduction by Mike Davis

The Paris Commune: A Revolution in Democracy
Donny Gluckstein

The Revolutionary Ideas of Karl Marx
Alex Callinicos

Rosa Luxemburg
Paul Frölich

The Spectre of Babeuf
Ian Birchall

Trotsky on Lenin
Leon Trotsky

The Women Incendiaries
Edith Thomas

ABOUT HAYMARKET BOOKS

Haymarket Books is a radical, independent, nonprofit book publisher based in Chicago.

Our mission is to publish books that contribute to struggles for social and economic justice. We strive to make our books a vibrant and organic part of social movements and the education and development of a critical, engaged, international left.

We take inspiration and courage from our namesakes, the Haymarket martyrs, who gave their lives fighting for a better world. Their 1886 struggle for the eight-hour day—which gave us May Day, the international workers' holiday—reminds workers around the world that ordinary people can organize and struggle for their own liberation. These struggles continue today across the globe—struggles against oppression, exploitation, poverty, and war.

Since our founding in 2001, Haymarket Books has published more than five hundred titles. Radically independent, we seek to drive a wedge into the risk-averse world of corporate book publishing. Our authors include Noam Chomsky, Arundhati Roy, Rebecca Solnit, Angela Davis, Howard Zinn, Amy Goodman, Wallace Shawn, Mike Davis, Winona LaDuke, Ilan Pappé, Richard Wolff, Dave Zirin, Keeanga-Yamahtta Taylor, Nick Turse, Dahr Jamail, David Barsamian, Elizabeth Laird, Amira Hass, Mark Steel, Avi Lewis, Naomi Klein, and Neil Davidson. We are also the trade publishers of the acclaimed Historical Materialism Book Series and of Dispatch Books.